Ultima Thule Publishing

12/21

DALTON DISCOVERY SERIES #2

Raining

Violets

The Complete Works

of

Robert Loveman

First Edition: February 2016

Copyright © 2016
Ultima Thule Publishing

ISBN-13: 978-0692642719

Cover Design: *Ethan W. Dempsey*
Interior Formatting: *Ethan W. Dempsey*

Printed in the United States of America

Books by Robert Loveman

Poems (1897)

A Book of Verses (1900)

The Gates of Silence (1903)

Songs from a Georgia Garden (1904)

The Blushful South and Hippocrene (1909)

On the Way to Willowdale (1912)

Sonnets of the Strife (1917)

Robert Loveman

Poems

Originally published in 1897

TABLE OF CONTENTS

2

To

MY SISTERS LINKA AND ANNE

MY JOSEPHINE

There was a France, there was a queen,
There was another Josephine,
Whose gentle love and tender art
Subdued Napoleon's soldier heart.

But she of France was ne'er, I ween,
Fairer than thou, my Josephine;
To storm thy heart I'll boldly plan,
God! If I were the Corsican!

OCTOBER

In April mortal's eye hath seen
The waking woods arrayed in green,
While every birdling of the throng
Essayed sweet syllables of song.

And now October wooes the wold
To dreams of crimson and of gold;
The laughing leaves, all out of breath,
Are dancing down to dusty death.

DREAMS

Dreams, like children hand in hand,
Wander through the shadow-land;
All the night they softly creep
Down the corridors of sleep.

Dreams, like children, laugh and weep
In the mystic house of sleep;
Then hand in hand they run away,
Frightened by the noisy day.

YON STAR

Yon star that glitters in the east
Shone o'er Belshazzar's fated feast,
Or lighted up the evening sky
For Esther and for Mordecai.

Yon star looking down with sleepless lids
Upon the rising pyramids,
And shall illume the final gust
That levels them to desert dust.

IN VENICE

In Venice, on the Rialto,
A merry mass of people go;
The siren city, like a bride,
Clings to the Adriatic's side;
By day, by night, one may still hear
The soft song of the gondolier,
Whose oar is strong for friend or foe,
In Venice, on the Rialto.

In Venice, on the Rialto,
Homesick and lone, I weep with woe;
Homesick and lone, what is to me
This marble city by the sea?
One vision all my bosom fills---
O village in the Georgia hills,
For thee my heart is bended low,
In Venice, on the Rialto.

NORTHPORT TOWN

In Northport town the sun goes down
Behind the hill, then all is still
With the peaceful village, where
A benison is in the air.
A pilgrim host of crickets yield
An Angelus for every field;
And there the moon looks kindly down
In mellow beams on Northport town.

In Northport town – her eyes are brown,
Her hair as soft as any down
On any dove whose liquid note
Of love is heard within the cote.
Ah, this thy secret, village fair!
Ah, this thy charm, O village rare!
Heaven, rain thy sweetest odors down,
For Lottie lives in Northport town.

IN NAISHÁPÚR

In Naishápúr, when Omar wrote,
No nightingale with lusty throat
Caroled a clearer, sweeter note
 In Naishápúr.

He saw the yellow roses swoon
Beneath the kisses of the June,
And the star blossoms of the night
Opened their petals to his sight.

He sang of life, and death, and of woe
A thousand years or so ago;
The north winds o'er him rose-leaves throw
 In Naishápúr.

UPON A CRUTCH

Upon a crutch, her girlish face
Alight with love and tender grace,
Laughing she limps from place to place,
    Upon a crutch.

And you and I, who journey through
A rose-leaf world of dawn and dew,
We cry to heaven overmuch,

We rail and frown at fate, while she,
And many more in agony,
Are brave and gentle, strong and true,
    Upon a crutch.

A "LA FRANCE" ROSE

Thou art the rarest regal rose
The Summer in her glory shows,
With golden honey on thy lips,
Patrician to thy petals' tips.

If thou hadst bloomed in Paris, when
The Commune thronged with frenzied men,
Some Robespierre plant by weeds begat
Had slain thee, sweet aristocrat.

FROM FOREIGN LANDS

From foreign lands the ships come in
And greet the city's cheerful din,
Laden with love or steeped with sin,
    From foreign lands.

Yonder a giant cruiser bides
And struggles with the surging tides;
While, ill from grief and penury,

Through all the long night's mystery
A lonely man looks out to sea
And weeps for home and Italy,
    From foreign lands.

CLEOPATRA

Egypt and Pharaoh and the Nile,
    A torrid vast of desert land,
Huge pyramids that grimly smile
    Across the shifting sand.

Egypt and Pharaoh, ay; but this---
    This Cleopatra wonders me,
Who leaped with many a burning kiss
    Into the arms of Antony.

11

THE VIGIL

Lest some sweet thought all unaware
Slip by me in the viewless air,
Lest some dear dream that softly stole
Past many a mighty poet-soul,

I'll in the morning sunshine sit,
And watch, and wait, and pray for it;
Naught else possess my mind or eye,
Lest some sweet thought slip slyly by.

O ISRAEL!

O Israel! thy glory gleamed
    Through ages long ago;
O Israel! a David dreamed
    Within thy tents of snow;
Thy warriors wise, and brave, and good,
Thy women queens of womanhood,
A pillared cloud and manna food,
    O Israel! sweet Israel!

O Israel! again I see
    Thy chariot in the sky!
The seed of Abraham shall be
    Through all eternity;
Our fathers' faith, our fathers' God,
The paths of peace wherein they trod,
With love, with truth, thy soul be shod,
    O Israel! sweet Israel!

FROM FAR JAPAN

From far Japan a pretty fan
Hath come my lady's joy to plan,
With rapture her sweet face to scan,
    From far Japan.

To touch the velvet of her hand
It journeyed over sea and land;
To flutter 'neath her lustrous eyes
Forsook the glow of Orient skies.

And yet I know it must be so,
The fan is happy. I would go,
For her, forever to and fro
    From far Japan.

TO-DAY'S RESOLVE

To-day no coward thought shall start
Upon its journey from my heart,
To-day no hasty word shall slip
Over the threshold of my lip.

To-day no selfish hope shall rest
Within the region of my breast,
To-day no wave of wrath shall roll
Over the ocean of my soul.

To-day I vow with sword and song
To fight oppression and the wrong,
To-day I dedicate my youth
To duty and eternal truth.

THE PARALYTIC

I.

He reads of the deeds of mighty men,
Of men in the brunt of battle, when,
With livid lips and bated breath
And loud huzzas, they dash to death.

II.

He reads of the deeds; his shrunken hands
Are tightly clinched; he understands
And feels, or why the storm
That rages through his helpless form?

THE WIND

I.

The wind came up from the balmy south,
  Came merrily dancing everywhere;
He kissed my lady's rose-bud mouth
  And slept in the coils of her shining hair.

II.

Then waked and away to the sobbing sea,
  Swifter than hungry hawk or fox,
And angrily dashed, with demonic glee,
  A giant ship against the rocks.

PURITY

Whose mind is pure, he is the man
For whom Almighty God doth plan;
For him in ecstasy the day
Doth blush itself in bliss away.

Whose heart is pure, for him the night
Visions and dreams of rare delight;
For him, beyond the sunset bars,
God sows the meadow sky with stars.

Whose soul is pure, for him the sea,
The mountain and its mystery;
For him, in all her shy retreats,
The tender heart of Nature beats.

Whose inmost thought, whose life is pure,
His soul is destined to endure,
To feel, to frame, to pray, to sing,
In gardens of God's blossoming.

O MOTHER MINE!

O mother mine! in other days,
Or ere I knew of blame or praise,
Thine was the love to light my ways,
    O mother mine!

And now, when Time, with tender touch,
Hath led thee gently down the years,
O mother mine! with tears, with tears,

I pray my care of thee be such
To pay in feeble part the debt,
If I have caused thee one regret,
    O mother mine!

OVER THE WAY

I.

Over the way, on a bending bough,
A joyous bird is singing now,
Into the heart of the summer day
Trilling a merry roundelay.

II.

And over the way the blinds are drawn,
A mother's hope and love is gone;
Without, the song, ---within, the gloom;
A babe lies dead in the darkened room.

NIAGARA

I.

Some vast despair, some grief divine,
    Doth vigil keep
Forever here; before this shrine
    The waters weep.

II.

Methinks a God from some far sphere,
    In sportive part,
In ages past wooed Nature here,
    And broke her heart.

19

THE TRUANT

I.

In the last twilight dim and gray
From my fond clasp she slipped away,
As sweet a thought as ever stole
Into and out a poet's soul.

II.

And now, through all the weary night,
Within my heart I burn a light,
So my dear thought may enter when
She cometh weeping home again.

HER MAJESTY

I.

The kingly Sun hath westward sped;
    Now cometh soon,
By planet princes heralded,
    The maiden Moon.

II.

And as unto the throne of night
    She draweth near,
Each courtier star, with paling light,
    Doth disappear.

TROUBLE TOWN

As I came down from Trouble Town
I met an angel on the way,
A radiant angel on the way;
She looked into my aching eyes,---
O angel good and true and wise!---
She whispered hope,---O vision rare!---
She bade me bravely burdens bear,
She kissed away each fading frown
As I came down from Trouble Town.

I'm glad I've been to Trouble Town,
Else might I ne'er have known or seen.
Oh, hast thou never known or seen,
When struggling back to life and hope,
The vision on some sunny slope,
With eager arms and eyes of light,
While once again the earth was bright?
God, it is good that, king or clown,
We all must go to Trouble Town.

TO LONDON TOWN

To London town Will Shakespeare went,
Ambitious, eager, and intent,
To one vast end his being bent,
              To London town.

He hugged his precious manuscript
Close to his heart, his fancy tripped
All feather-footed through the day.

And she---poor, lone Ann Hathaway---
Taught Judith, Hamnet, how to pray
For him---her lord, away, away
              To London town.

SWEET ARE THE NAMES

Sweet are the names and Shakespeare's women, they
Like music melt upon the heart and ear;
First Juliet comes, then Beatrice draws near,
Perdita pure, and Lucrece chaste as day,
Dear Desdemona, she who loved the Moor,
There, poor Ophelia, and Cordelia here,
Whose voice was ever soft and low to Lear;
Rare Rosalind, the fair who reigned o'er
Orlando's soul in Arden, Portia wise,
And Jessica, who with an unthrift love
Ran far as Belmont; look your last now, eyes,
On maid Miranda, gentle as a dove.
These names and women out of Shakespeare's art,
Like sweetest music, sway the human heart.

A SUNRISE

Up from the under wonder-world,
    A thousand battles won,
The east hath every flag unfurled:
    Good-morning, Signor Sun!

A SUNSET

A crimson, gray, and gold
    Enchantment to the eye;
Some artist saint spilled all his paint
    Adown the western sky.

POOR LITTLE ROSE

I know you, rose; I see you there,
Bathed in the balmy April air;
I've watched the weary winter through,
And seen the sun smile down on you,
Seen day by day your leaves grow green,
And baby buds spring up between;
So now small wonder that I feel
Thy charm, my mellow Maréchal Niel.
I know you, rose; your heart is won
By your fond love, the summer sun;
You sigh for him the long night through,
At morn your cheek is wet with dew,
With tears of dew, sweet loyal rose,
For oh, the night so slowly goes!
But when your lover sails the sky,
Ah, then again your cheek is dry,
And so I know your soul is won
By your fond love, the summer sun;
And yet, poor rose, ere many days,
Beneath his ardent burning rays,
E'en while he lightens earth and sky,
Thou then, sad queen, must drooping die,
And then he'll amorous glances throw
Upon some jaunty Jacqueminot,
And her torn heart will also feel

All thou hast known, my Maréchal Niel---
All of thy joys, all of thy woes,
Poor little rose,---poor little rose.

THE FREEBOOTER

Drunken with dew, a bandit bee
    Across my flower-garden goes;
The noisy knave, what recketh he
    To stab a bettle, rob a rose?

IN AUTUMN

The shepherd winds are driving
    Along the ways on high
A merry flock of cloudland sheep
    To meadows in the sky.

VERLAINE, VILLON, BAUDELAIRE

Verlaine, Villon, Baudelaire,
Delicacy and despair,
Perfume, poison, myrrh, and rue,
Bitter-sweet and honey-dew,
Lurid skies and absinthe air,
Verlaine, Villon, Baudelaire.

Verlaine, Villon, Baudelaire,
Chansonnette and rondeau rare,
Ballade, quatrain, villanelle,
Lovingly they wrought and well;
A fig for grief and carking care,
Verlaine, Villon, Baudelaire.

Verlaine, Villon, Baudelaire,
The pity of it,---everywhere

POETRY

O art of arts! O gift of gifts!
       Sublimest of sublime!
To string the beaded thoughts into
       A rosary of rhyme.

WHERE DREAM-BOATS DRIFT

Over the silver sea of sleep
       The dream-boats drift away, away,
Adown the dawn they softly creep
       Into the harbor of the day

WORDS

Words, words, words
That bubble up from baby lips,
Or falter trembling forth when age
Upon the homeward journey slips
And stumbles; words that rise
In prayer like incense to the skies,
Words that light with love the page,
Words, words, words.

Words, words, words
That poets borrow from the birds,
Willing words that have been caught
To the bosom of a thought;
Words of honey, words of gall,
Words that hold the heart in thrall,
Words sublime that chime and rhyme,
Words, words, words.

THE ANGELUS

This scene I see, this thought I feel,
    Ah, distant days are glowing there,
When Millet's mother bade him kneel
    And lisp in love his evening prayer.

THE MUSE

No sooner doth one song depart,
    In fancy's realm to soar,
Another stands outside my heart
    And taps upon the door.

ROSE IS THE GIRL

Rose is the girl; she bids me write
A rhyme for her, and I am quite
At loss for language adequate.
   Rose is the girl.

She is my life, my love, my fate,
To her my dreams are dedicate,
And when the moon shall shine to-night

I'll hie me to my lady's bower
And swear allegiance by the hour.
O Venus, Cupid, give me power!
   Rose is the girl.

A DREAMER

He is a dreamer, let him pass,
He reads the writing in the grass;
His seeing soul in rapture goes
Beyond the beauty of the rose.
He is a dreamer, and doth know
To sound the farthest depth of woe;
His days are calm, majestic, free;
He is a dreamer, let him be.

He is a dreamer; all the day
Blest visions throng him on his way,
Past the far sunset and the light,
Beyond the darkness and the night.
He is a dreamer---God! to be
Apostle of Infinity,
And mirror truth's translucent gleam;
He is a dreamer, let him dream.

He is a dreamer; for all time
His mind is married unto rhyme,
Light that ne'er was on land or sea
Hath blushed to him in poetry.
He is a dreamer, and hath caught
Close to his heart a hope, a thought,---
A hope of immortality;

He is a dreamer, let him be.

He is a dreamer; lo! with thee
His soul doth weep in sympathy;
He is a dreamer, and doth long
To glad the world with happy song.
He is a dreamer---in a breath
He dreams of love, and life, and death.
Oh man! Oh woman! lad and lass,
He is a dreamer, let him pass.

UP TO THE REALM

Up to the realm where she doth reign,
    Unto its utmost holy height,
Through all the muse's dear domain,
    The poet's path is one of light.

But if the way were bleak and long,
    And from the night no friendly spark,
To see her face---O child of song!---
    Who would not leap into dark?

THE GALAXY

The Night is soon to wed the Day,
And for the virgin pale
Hath wrought a multitude of stars
Into a bridal veil.

BEFORE THE STORM

The old oak wakes from peaceful sleep,
Roused by the earth's alarms,
And frightened baby breezes leap
Into his outstretched arms.

QUATRAIN

The night is a moonlit garden,
    The night is a starry feast,
And the white-rose Sun, at dawning,
    Unfolds his petals in the east.

QUATRAIN

God made the Night, and marveling how
    That she might be most ravishingly fair,
He orbed the moon upon her beauteous brow,
    And meshed a myriad of stars within her hair.

BOHEMIA

Bohemia is the land for me;
    Its mountains tower heaven high,
Its singing rivers seek the sea,
    Its cloud-craft sail the ocean sky;
Out of the close embrace of Night,
    Burning with blushes, comes the Dawn;
Bohemia hath the rarer light,---
    The light that leads the poet on.

Bohemia is the land for me;
    There Shakespeare, Milton, Byron, Keats
Plucked from its heart the mystery,
    Walked in its ways and rapt retreats;
It is a land whose splendors smite
    When sun and moon and stars are gone,
It is the land where shines the light,---
    The light that leads the poet on.

Bohemia is the land for me;
    It is the purple land of dreams,
Where on may quaff the nectary
    Of noble thoughts and lofty themes;
Through Sorrow hath a cheek of white
    And Hunger's face be pinched and wan,

Dear God! the more we love the light,---
The light that leads the poet on.

Bohemia is the land for me;
It is the rosy realm of rhyme,
Of music, art, and ecstasy,
It is the clime of deeds sublime;
And o'er it all by day and night,
And past the portals of the dawn,
The gleaming, beaming, streaming, light
Shall ever lead the poet on.

SERENADE

Good-night, the day has slipped to sleep;
   Good-night, my love, good-night;
The stars are tears the heavens weep;
   Good-night, my love, good-night.
Sweetness and beauty, goodness, grace,
And happiness are in thy face;
Where thou art hallowed is the place;
   Good-night, my love, good-night.

Good-night, once more upon my breast,
   Good-night, my love, good-night;
My heart the haven, stay and rest;
   Good-night, my love, good-night.
Sweetheart, my own, or ere I go,
Once more,---dear love, I love thee so,
Once more___O ecstasy of woe!
   Good-night, my love, good-night.

CHARLOTTE CORDAY

The canvas speaks; again we see
Marat in death's dark agony;
Again the throng whose weeping eyes
Saw thy pure spirit seek the skies.

The canvas speaks; behind the bars,
Immortal as the steadfast stars,
Thy soul still shines with holy light,
Kindled in Revolution's night.

The canvas speaks; away! away!
In cloisters hooded friars pray
Repose to one who drew the lance
From out the bleeding breast of France.

The canvas weeps; adieu! adieu!
Forever live the brave and true;
Music and marble, brush and rhyme,
Treasure the memory for all time.

TO LIFT MEN UP

To lift men up, oh, this mine aim,---
Away with pomp and pride and fame,---
Through light and darkness, fire and flame,
    To lift men up.

Dear God! for me no crown or state,
No love alone for low or great,
But for one vast humanity,

With hearts as restless as the sea,
And souls serene through suffering;
For them, for these, still let me sing,
    To lift men up.

ON THE FLY-LEAF

Here find we peace and tumult, hope, despair,
Now feel we winter's wind, now Arden's air;
There vice its curse as Caliban doth show
Next maid Miranda, chaste as virgin snow;
This page a scene of cruel carnage brings,
And this, a bridal bed---that couch, a king's;
Cordelia's eye holds pity's melting tear
E'en while the howling tempest echoes Lear.
O might soul! who in one fleeting breath
Could picture hell and heaven, life and death,
Base-born the slave who can thy precepts quote
And thank not God a Shakespeare lived and wrote.

A COMFORTER

Vexed with the trials of a dismal day,
    I sat me down to rail at God and man,
To pour into a bitter venomed lay
    All vile anathema, a curse, a ban;
Hope seemed to stumble on her weary way,
    And a dark purpose like a river ran
Through my sad soul. But how, oh, friend, I pray,
    Can one long murmur at the ordained plan,
When to the haven of his arms there slips
    A baby daughter robed in snowy white,
Who, with love's prattle on her infant lips,
    Has come to kiss and bid me sweet good-night,
And whispers, cuddling close her precious head,
"I'm sleepy, papa; come, put me to bed?"

THIS WINTER NIGHT

This winter night, against the pane,
I hear the beating of the rain;
The mad wind shrieks a harsh refrain
    This winter night.

Within my room, in warmth and light,
The friendly fire blazes bright,
And---God! out in the bitter cold

How many mortals wander on,
With love and hope and gladness gone,
Poor human sheep outside the fold,
    This winter night!

ROMEO AND JULIET

I.

O Moon, didst thou see, that night, sweet night,
    'Neath thy mellow beams and the stars aglow,
Juliet, with eyes of love and light,
    Close in the arms of Romeo?

II.

And, Moon, hast thou seen the night, sad night,
    When Verona ran with bated breath,
And wept at the cruel, piteous sight
    Of the ill-starred pair in the arms of death?

WHEREFORE?

When no sweet thoughts will come to thee
    And harbor in thy heart,
When no dear dreams of ecstasy
    Will woo thy lips apart;

When no rose-rhyme shall bloom for thee
    In gardens God doth give,
Though thine the all of land and sea,
    Wherefore, O poet, live?

44

THE RAIN

O the rain, the summer rain,
Kissing all the growing grain,
And the sudden little showers
Giving fragrance to the flowers!
Every streamlet runs along
With a sweeter, clearer song,
To the river, then the main.
O the rain, the rain, the rain!

O the rain, the winter rain,
Beating through the broken pane,
Where with weary heart and brain
Many weep in vain, in vain!
Poor, so poor that hope is dead,
And the children cry for bread.
God, the sorrow! God, the strain!
O the rain, the rain, the rain!

GOOD-BY

We say at noon and in the night,
    Good-by, good-by, good-by;
Thought tears at parting blind the sight,
    Good-by, good-by, good-by.
Over the vasty deep we go
Unto a land afar, and lo!
One little word to tell the woe,
    Good-by, good-by, good-by.

To father, mother, husband, wife,
    Good-by, good-by, good-by;
Love is the guiding star of life,
    Good-by, good-by, good-by.
After the death let come what may,
Our deeds shall live for aye and aye,
And consecrate our peaceful clay,
    Good-by, good-by, good-by.

A LYRIC

A lyric, love, for you, my love,
A lyric; words that weep
And thoughts that pray shall creep
Into my song and kneel to thee.
For you, my love, a lyric.

A lyric, love, for you, my love,
A lyric; oh, sweetly slain am I;
One dagger glance from thy dark eye
Hath done the deed---I swoon, I die.
For you, my love, a lyric.

A lyric, love, for you, my love,
A lyric; all the south
Hath not the honey of thy mouth,
The beauty of thy bosom, love.
For you, my love, a lyric.

A lyric, love, for you, my love,
A lyric; soul of mine,
Never had mortal sweeter shrine
Than where I worship, while I sing
For you, my love, a lyric.

HE IS NOT OLD

He is not old whose eyes are bright,
Whose bosom throbs, whose heart is light;
Though fourscore be his years enrolled,
If yet he loves, he is not old.
O'er him whose inmost thought is true
The sky of winter beameth blue;
For if a man have heart of gold,
Though white his hair, he is not old.

Age only rests upon the throng
Who live in strife, who cherish wrong;
For oh, 'tis vice that makes us cold,
And then, alas! we soon grow old.
So, friend, and thou wouldst be
A man of mirth, not misery,
Be just and gentle, brave and bold,
And then thou never need'st be old.

IN LIGHTER VEIN

In lighter vein, one might indite
To Preciosa something trite,
Liken her eyes to stars of night,
    In lighter vein.

In lighter vein; but softly stay:
When one doth writhe in grievous pain,
With fevered brow and burning brain,

When shadows chase the sun away,
And every infant hope is slain,
How can one write, I pray, I pray,
    In lighter vein?

THE PLAY IS O'ER

The play is o'er! my lady wept
The last act through; Othello crept
To Desdemona's feet and died.
O maddened Moor---ill-fated bride,
     The play is o'er!

Homeward we go, while music sweet
Still haunts our ears; across the street
Two shots ring out---the tramp of feet.

They hastily bear away
On one rude couch the lifeless clay.
A jealous fool---his mistress gay,
     The play is o'er!

IN OLDEN TIME

In olden time a bonny maid,
A cavalier and his cockade,
A bit of sunshine and of shade
    In olden time.

He wooed the winsome woman till
She yielded to his sovereign will,
And to the farthest gates of death

Love, love was their sweet shibboleth;
And happiness and joy untold
Blossomed within their hearts of gold
    In olden time.

SOME WORDS

Some words there be of infamy,
    And others dearer than delight;
Some whiter than a June noonday;
    Some blacker than a starless night;

Some---but for me can never be
Lute notes of sweeter ecstasy
Than those fond words of love that drip
Like honey from my lady's lip.

SONNET

Drunk with delight, the rose I gave her dreams
Upon the billowed bosom of my love;
It falls and rises with the waves thereof,
And hath forgot the Sun-God's ardent beams;
A softer summer now doth compass it,
At anchor in the harbor of her heart.
No more for thee, O rose! the night starlit,
Dawn's magic, or the noontide's golden art,
But rarer rapture shall these joys eclipse
If she absolve thee once with her sweet lips.
Oh, thy blissful destiny were mine,
    To drink the heavy honey of her breath,
Feel for one day her touch, her clasp divine,
    Sink into sleep and swoon to glorious death.

A DIAMOND

Look how it sparkles, see it greet
    With laughing light the ambient air;
One little drop of sunshine sweet
    Held in eternal bondage there.

CARCASSONNE

The land of love, the land of light,
    The Canaan never cursed with care,
Lies just beyond---so poets write---
    The sunless sea of dark despair.

INTO THE POET'S LIFE

Into the poet's life one day
A sorrow came in ashen gray,
Into his life a sorrow came
And bowed his head with grief and shame.
It dimmed the lustre of his eye
And stole the sunlight from the sky,
Trampled the tender shoots of truth
And sacked the temple of his youth.

Out of the poet's soul one day
A song of courage sped away,
A song of comfort, hope, and cheer,
Born of a doubt, a sob, a tear,---
Out of his soul, on eagle wing.
O poet rare! thy suffering,
As well as joy, shall light for thee
The ways to immortality.

NOT THOU

God, let me write a rhyme so pure
    That men who read will pray,---
A poem pure that will endure
    Unto the latest day!

This my heart's hope, but on a scroll
    Unfolded to my sight
I read, "Not thou, whose secret soul
    Is damned and black as night!"

WHEN THE MOOD IS ON

When the mood is on, oh, the cunning then,
And the rapture rare of the poet's pen!
The singing soul soars away, away,
And the happy heart hath holiday.
The sky is clear, all the clouds are gone,
When the mood is on, when the mood is on.
When the mood is on, from the earth to sky,
In a frenzy fine rolls the poet's eye;
He hath no sorrow, he hath no care,
A spirit of joy is everywhere;
"Tis a golden day with diamond dawn,
When the mood is on, when the mood is on.
When the mood is on, to the western Ind
No jewel fair as Rosalind,
And all learn lessons true and good
From the rocks and trees of the Arden wood;
"Tis an age of beauty, brain, and brawn,
When the mood is on, when the mood is on.
But soft, there are faces pinched and drawn
And hearts that bleed when the mood is on;
There are those who weep beside their dead,
There are hungry hosts who cry for bread
Through the long long night and alas! the dawn,
When the mood is on, when the mood is on.

IN SHAKESPEARE LAND

In Shakespeare Land are sylvan scenes,
Hills heaven high and broad demesnes,
Princes, courtiers, kings, and queens
    In Shakespeare Land.

Tybalt is there and Romeo;
"Consort us," quoth Mercutio;
"Have at the villain" so-and-so.

Now, nurse, to gentle Juliet go
And bid her weep and fast and pray;
Woe, woe betide the fatal day
    In Shakespeare Land!

SOLE EMPRESS

A thousand dreams of duty haunt my heart,
    A thousand passions beat about my brain,
An ocean-tide of fragrant fancies start
    And burn my being with exquisite pain.

These and a million more besieging things
    Seek to invade my bosom's citadel,
Where she---my lady---reigns supreme and sings,
    Her smile my heaven and her frown my hell.

THE MUSICIAN

The earth, the sky, the land and sea
For him make sweetest melody;
He hears the faintest flowing note
That ripples from the linnet's throat.

A STORMY NIGHT

All night the waves of darkness roar
And break against a starless shore,
All night---then, weary, spent, and wan,
They die upon the dikes of dawn.

A PRAYER

Not faith and hope and charity
      Alone secure the soul's success;
O ye immortal Gods, to me
      Give fearlessness, give fearlessness!

RESOLUTION

O God, for strength to turn
    Our souls to ventures vast!
And, pressing on, behind us burn
    The bridges of the past.

THE POET

Most might of magicians he
Who, with some subtle sorcery,
Can kiss a cold, forbidding truth
To beauty and immortal youth.

A DERELICT

An ocean outcast, baffled, blown
    By every wind and wave;
In death not even poor "Unknown"
    Above his lonely grave.

ADOWN THE YEARS

Perhaps I may
     Have gone amiss,
To steal one day
     From her a kiss;
But heaven knows
     I'd suffer pain
And direst woes
     To kiss again.
"Twas long ago,
     And yet I vow
It thrilled me so
     It seems as now,
And through the mist
     Of many years
The girl I kissed
     I see in tears.
That she should cry
     And rail at fate
Was more than I
     Dare contemplate;
So on that day,
     Adown the years,
I kissed away
     Her pretty fears.

Sing, poet, sing
    Of what you will,
The sweetest thing
    Is love's first thrill;
And, of all joys,
    The height of bliss
Is but a boy's
    First loving kiss.

LOOKING SEAWARD

I.

Thy breasted billows rise and fall,
    O breathing sea!
Some joy doth hold thy soul in thrall
    Of ecstasy.

II.

And so, my love, my life, my sweet,
    Whate'er may be,
Thus should thy billowed bosom beat
    At thought of me.

HER SOUL IS PURE

Her soul is pure and sweet and white;
  All good is garnered there;
If I might once peep in and write,
  What poem half so fair?

When next across my path she trips,
  This woman wondrous wise,
I'll kiss a lyric from her lips,
  An epic from her eyes.

SO DARK, SO DEAR

Death is so dark to youth,
  So cruel, dank, and drear;
Ambition, love, and truth
  All buried in the bier.

Death is so dear to age,
  So sweet the peace and rest;
Nor summer's heat nor winter's rage,
  Hands folded o'er the breast.

TO MY MOTHER

Many the weary miles between,
    But distance yields to love like thine.
Blest miracle! though all unseen,
    Closely thy cheek is pressed to mine.

A SUNSET

The Sun, departing, kissed the summer Sky,
    Then ben an instant o'er her beating breast;
She lifts to him a timid, tear-stained eye,
    And lo! her blushes crimson all the west.

FAITH

Oceans nor mountains do I need
    To thunder wisdom down to me;
The drop of dew, the living seed,
    All whisper of Infinity.

INSPIRATION

Joy now hath reached her utmost goal
And sunrise bursts upon the soul
When some immortal thought or plan
Runs riot in the mind of man.

SOMEWHERE, AFAR

Somewhere, afar, dear God, we know
    The mountain-height of glory gleams,
For some fame's fragrant breezes blow
    Across the meadow-land of dreams.

THE QUATRAIN

Only four scanty lines are there,
    Yet might a master-mind rehearse
All heaven's hope and hell's despair
    Within one little, trembling verse.

EMANCIPATION

Grandeur and truth, infinite grace,
And love shine from his kingly face;
Now doth man's visage pure and fair
Reflect God's imaged glory there.

THE HOME-COMING

Through all the day the witching words
    Elude the poet's art,
Till eve; then winged thoughts, like birds,
    Fly homeward to his heart.

MAN

The vilest creature space doth span
Is weak, despised, dishonored man;
The crown of God's immortal plan,
Noble and lofty, fearless man.

ACTION

I know not how some men can lie
In ease and inactivity,
When Nature's children all uplift
Their voices in a song of thrift.

QUATRAIN

Weak from its war with giant strife,
    A struggling truth lay down to die;
A poet loved it back to life
    And gave it immortality

DARKNESS

Stumbling along the ways through space,
    Led by the wanton wind,
No light illumes his furrowed face,---
    The old man Earth is blind!

THE SANCTUM SANTORUM

Guard well the temple of the mind,
   Its portals keep with care;
No pilgrim thought impure, unkind,
   Should ever enter there.

HER

Hair like to melted midnight,
   And her eyes,---O God, her eyes!
The lips of language ne'er have loosed
   Words worthy their sweet witcheries.

IF THOU WOULDST READ

If thou wouldst read his verse aright,
Deem it a cry from out the night;
No idle theme is penciled there,
It is his soul's immortal prayer.

THE POET

Through the sweet summer of his years,
Wherever blossom hopes and fears,
He doth pursue his magic art
And hives the honey in his heart.

IN THE YOSEMITE

The centuries have builded here,
　　O'er many a rugged rod
Of peak and cave, a temple where
　　Nature might worship God.

A THOUGHT

　　My kingdom for a thought!
One deathless thought, one thought to reach
The utmost bounds of human speech;
　　My kingdom for a thought!

THE MOB

A surging sea of maddened men,
   Curses and cries, that rise and fall;
The stillness of the grave---and then
   King Death will hold high carnival.

THE DAWN

Upon his tranquil, joyous face
Sorrow hath left no dark'ning trace,
And yet we know the blessed light
Followed a struggle in the night.

MARCH

Whither doth now this fellow flee
   With outstretched arms at such mad pace?
Can the young rascal thinking be
   To catch a glimpse of April's face?

APRIL

Maiden, thy cheeks with tears are wet,
    And ruefully thine eyebrows arch;
Is't as they say, thou thinkest yet
    Of that inconstant madcap March?

SHE IS

Gentle and tender, sweet and true,
Calm as a summer sky of blue,
And in the depths of her dark eyes
Passion, the tiger, couchant lies.

SPRING

A whisper on the heath I hear,
    And blossoms deck the waking wood;
Ah! surely now the virgin year
    Is in her blushing maidenhood.

OVERHEARD

I lingered listening 'neath the tree,
   The summer sky above me,
And when a sunbeam kissed a leaf,
   It whispered low, "I love thee."

NIGHT

The Empress Night hath jewels rare
Of diamond stars within her hair,
And on her beauteous bosom soon
She'll wear the silver crescent moon.

THE END.

A

Book

of

Verses

Originally published in 1900

To

LILLIAN AND EARNEST LOVEMAN

TABLE OF CONTENTS

DEAR LITTLE VERSE

Dear little verse, the careless eye
And heedless heart will pass thee by,
And never needst thou hope to be
To others as thou art to me.

For lo, I know thy bliss and woe,
Thy shallows, depths, and boundless heights,
How thou wast wrought, patient and slow,
Through crucibles of sleepless nights.

THE CRUISE

The crescent moon's a yellow boat
    Upon the evening sea,
And every little star afloat
    Doth bear her company.

Nightly they cruise their ocean o'er,
    Until, the darkness gone,
They anchor by some silent shore,
    Upon the isle of dawn.

SONG

When song-bird thoughts within his heart
    Make melody sublime,
The Poet snares them by his art
    Into a cage of rhyme.

And there the captive fancies beat
    There wings against the bars,
The music, soft and low and sweet,
    Ascending to the stars.

Yet evermore they long to be
    Back where the surges roll,
Untamed, unfettered, wild and free,
    Within the Poet's soul.

POMPEII

Pompeii sat smiling in the sun,
    She was a city young and fair,
The loved, the cherished, chosen one
    Of grim Vesuvius tow'ring there.

Pompeii woke trembling in the night,
    O livid night of lava sweat!
She hung her head to shut the sight,
    And in her terror hideth yet.

LINES AT SEA

We understand the leagues of land,
    The mountain and the vale,
The desert's hush, the meadow's blush,
    The jungle and the trail.

But all the sea is mystery,
    From farthest shore to shore,
Where white ships trip, and slip, and dip,
    And dance across her floor.

81

AN EXILE

I am an exile, in disgrace,
And sorrow banished from her face:
    Now some such woe as mine, I ween,
    Napoleon knew at Saint Helene.

I am an exile, fettered, ta'en
To deserts drear of her disdain;
    Will pity ne'er her bosom stir
    For my high crime of loving her?

ONE DAY

Up the empurpled east behold
    The royal squadron of the sun,
O'er ocean skies of blue and gold,
    The daily pilgrimage begun.

Across the noon, and far away,
    Asail on an imperial quest,
Until the fleets at anchor lay
    In some still harbor down the west.

OUTWARD BOUND

When I am outward bound at last,
    About my couch I pray,
No ghosts of sins from out my past
    Will drive my peace away.

I trust none come from out those years,
    And my departure see,
Or whisper in my dying ears,
    "Dost thou remember me?"

WITH OMAR IN THE ORIENT

I leave the western world to-day,
And ever eastward bear away
To tropic Persia's land of palm,
Of attar, aloe, myrrh, and balm;
Across the mountain and the sea,
My Pegasus shall carry me,
Until I breathe the bloom and scent,
With Omar in the Orient.
His nightingale will sing to me
All of the olden melody,
The wind will rifle gardens sweet,
And rain the roses at my feet;
His verses underneath the bough,
The loaf of bread, the wine,---and Thou,
All in one dream, beauty blent,
With Omar in the Orient.
Away with sorrow, grief, and care,
O, Saki, love and peace are there;
Away with all the ghostly fears
That low-browed Superstition rears;
Parwin, Mushtari, softly shine,
And light me onward to the shrine,
Where I may pitch my happy tent,
With Omar in the Orient.

TO HER

Her mind's a garden, where do grow
Sweet thoughts like posies in a row;

Her soul is as some lucent star,
That shines upon us from afar;

Her heart's an ocean, wide and deep,
Where swirling waves of passion sweep,

Aye, deeper than the deepest sea,
And wide as woman's mystery:

O man, the mariner, beware---
Yet will I chance a shipwreck there.

AERE PERENNIUS

Nations and men may pass away;
    A fragrant thought can never die;
The soul beneath its potent sway
    Ascends on high.

Poet, if thy dear verse doth hold
    Fast in its heart one truth sublime,
There shall it gleam, a star of gold,
    And outlive time.

SONG

Love is hot, and love is cold,
Love is gentle, love is bold,
Love can perish in a day,
O and love can last away;
Love hath rived my heart in twain,
Love hath healed the hurt again,
      O sweet Love!

Love is heaven, love is hell,
A dream, a truth, a miracle;
Love doth ripple like a rill,
Love can roar the torrent still;
How can weakling words portray,
That which over all hath sway,
      O sweet Love!

MY SOUL WAS THIRSTY

My soul was thirsty till she came,
    My heart was hungry till her eyes
Lighted love's fuel into flame
    And taught me Paradise.

I hunger and I thirst no more;
    Lo, 'tis a fount where honey drips;
I drink a thousand kisses from
    The chalice of her curved lips.

IN ENGLAND

This is the England, this is the earth,
That gave majestic Milton birth;
This is the olden golden clime
Of lofty prose, of lifting rhyme;
Here Poesy's pure soul was won
By the sweet strains of Tennyson;
For him her eyes knew no eclipse,
And he might kiss her lyric lips;
This is great England; here was wrought
The noblest monument of thought
That man e'er builded up to God
Out of his bosom's sacred sod,
For this the soil, and this the clime,
That gave a Shakespeare to all time.

BEHIND THE SCENES

Behind the scenes the kings and queens
Are merely mortals; Juliet leans,
A tired girl, against the screens,
      Behind the scenes.

The final act is on, and lo!
The loving heart of Romeo
Must crack with misery and woe;
The noble Paris, too, shall die,

And tears spring up in every eye;
Then exit all, while rouge and saint
Are scrubbing off the mask of paint,
      Behind the scenes.

THE RIDE

Little fellow, come to me,
For a ride upon my knee;
Here we go, so brisk and bright,
Through the village of Delight,
Up the happy hill of Joy,---
Goodness, what a heavy boy!
Down through Merry, Cheery Lane,
Now we gallop home again.

What a canter we have had,
You and I, my laughing lad!
Such sport one may only see
On a tried and trusted knee;
There, dismount, thou roguish sprite,
Hitch the horse up good and tight;
Next time we will take a run
Round the bailiwick of Fun.

PARIS

This is Paris, *s'il vous plait,*---
Careless, debonair, and gay,
Love and laughter, song and shout,
Women, wine, and merry bout.

This is Paris, *le voice,*---
Music, mirth, and misery,
Art divine, and sodden shame,
Glory, poverty, and fame.

This is Paris, *ècoutez,*---
After night must come the day,
Weak, inconstant, yea, accurst,
Folly's bubble soon will burst.

HEINE

A mattress grave, poor stricken Jew,
For years his broken body knew,
His pale brow wet with deadly dew,
    A mattress grave.

Below his prison place of pain,
Thronged all the gay Parisian train,
And helpless in his attic room,
Of anguish, agony, and gloom.

This wounded soul of song and wit,
Pressed wearily through days of doom,
O, pity, grief, and woe of it,
    A mattress grave!

PROCLAMATION

Robin in the red cravat,
    When winter days are done,
A memorial meeting to
    Emily Dickinson.

The humming-bird and butterfly
    Will tell of her and weep,
But she can never heed them,
    "Being just asleep."

CYRANO SPEAKS

I, Cyrano de Bergerac,
Can have nor sleep, nor peace, alack!
In my poor semblance now they rage,
And fiercely strut upon the stage.
The actors are a worthy crew,---
Coquelin and Irving, Mansfield too.
I bid them all go hang and pack,---
I, Cyrano de Bergerac.

I, Cyrano de Bergerac,
The mimic world upon my track,
Ah, rare Roxanne, before all men
We are impaled on Rostand's pen.
Once every tumult filled my breast,
And now they will not let me rest,
But I am dragged, unwilling, back,---
I, Cyrano de Bergerac.

SONG

When nights are calm, and days are dear,
    What can one do but sing?
When happiness is everywhere,
    What can one do but sing?
The mountains melt along the sky,
The snowy pigeons circling fly,
A thousand visions kiss the eye,---
    What can one do but sing?

When hope is thronèd in the heart,
    What can one do but sing?
When pity pleads, and sweet tears start,
    What can one do but sing?
A thousand lights are in the sky,
A thousand thoughts about me fly,
A thousand visions kiss mine eye,---
    What can one do but sing?

THE HEART OF GOD IN NATURE

I bear no ill to any hill,
    I'm brother to the trees,
My mind doth melt to mountains,
    And my soul doth seek the seas;
I greet the sun uprising
    With a friendly, loving nod;
Within the breast of Nature
    Throbs the heart of God.

To me a star is not afar,
    The moon doth know my face,
I often dream beneath her beam,
    And sue her sovereign grace;
The sky and air are very fair---
    Queen rose and golden-rod;
Within the breast of Nature
    Throbs the heart of God.

A little day, and then away,
    Unto another shore;
Some hasting years of bliss and tears,
    Then Charon at the oar;
Whatever cometh after
    Our sojourn 'neath the sod,
Within the breast of Nature
    Throbs the heart of God.

RICHES

What to a man who loves the air
Are trinkets, gauds, and jewels rare?
And what is wealth or fame to one
Who is a brother to the sun;
Who drinks the wine that morning spills
Upon the heaven-kissing hills,
And sees a ray of hope afar
In every glimmer of a star?

What to a man whose god is truth
Are spoils and stratagems, forsooth---
Who looks beyond the doors of death
For loftier life, sublime breath;
Who can forswear the state of kings
In knowledge of diviner things,
The dreams immortal that unroll
And burst to blossom in his soul?

THE SECRET

Of one great secret Omar knew
Little as I, as much as you;
And Shakespeare's soul and Milton's brain
Perplexèd paused at death's domain.

Dear God, who gave us thought and breath,
Divulge the mystery of death!
What suns shall light, what waters lave,
The mystic shores beyond the grave?

THE SIREN CITY

Paris sparkles as she lies,
    All unbosomed to the sun;
For the prize within her eyes
    Battles have been lost and won.
She is haughty, she is vain;
In her arms the serpent Seine,
And with wooing, cooing wiles,
Paris dazzles, Paris smiles.

Paris hath a mighty heart,
    Siren of the cities she,
Nobly wedded unto Art,
    Music, Marble, Poetry;
Heedless, happy, night and day,
She doth dance the years away.
With her graces and her guiles,
Paris loves, and dreams, and smiles.

À L'OPERA

Music swells my sluggish blood
To a raging purple flood,
Music rainbows on my brain
All the vanished years again.

Music in my soul doth stir
Sleeping memories of her;
Can nor time, nor any art,
Drive this woman from my heart?

THE PICTURES

This Corot is the "Ville D'Avray,"
That Rousseau is a prayer in gray,
The Inness "Landscape" seems to me
A spot I knew in Normandy.

Here is Fromentin's "Oasis,"
"Jeanne D'Arc" by rare Rosetti this,
And now a Troyon, happy chance,
That it should be, his "Coast of France."

Van Dyck, Fortuny, Ziem, Duprè,
All in immortal, brave array;
This last is living flesh aglow,
Breathed from the brush of Bouguereau.

SONG

When I an infant, peaceful lay
   Upon my loving Mother's breast,
She softly sung me, night and day,
   Sweet lullabies of faith and rest.

Through all my youth, through all my years,
   Her gentle songs have followed me,
The tender fountain of my tears
   Leaps up at their dear melody.

So all my days are days of song,
   And when shall come my life's eclipse,
O happy fate, to drift along
   To death with songs upon my lips.

LINES

I owe no map allegiance,
 I am prince, I'm king, I'm czar,
My courier winds bring odors
 From Arabian fields afar;
I drink the wine of sunset,
 I drain the cup of noon,
December is a bliss to me,
 An ecstasy is June.

The morning is a rapture,
 The midnight is a mood,
I sit at feasts of fancy,
 Where Gods confer the food;
And then the vision passes,
 From joy to grief and gloom,---
And I see a Poet dying
 In a narrow little room.

LULLABY

Slip away to Slumber Land,
    Baby, O, my baby,
Weary little foot and hand,
    Baby, O, my baby;
You shall have a rattle, and
A wooly dog, a dragon grand:---
Finest fellow in the land,
    Baby, O, my baby.

Cuddle down and close your eyes,
    Baby, O, my baby,
See how snugly there he lies,
    Baby, O, my baby;
Stars are peeping from the skies,---
How one so young can be so wise,
Is mightiest of mysteries,
    Baby, O, my baby.

IF HONOR STAY

All is not gone if Honor stay,
Though friends forsake, and foes betray,
Though torture rend thee limb from limb,
And faith is dead, and hope is dim.

If on thy bosom's sacred throne,
The Truth doth reign, supreme, alone,
Away! thou bauble Life, away!
Nothing is gone if Honor stay.

THE POET'S REALM

Little fortune hath the Bard
But a store of coined kisses,
Who can deem his doom so hard
When the Matrons and the Misses
Pay him for songs with blisses?
They are taken with his eyes
And his saint-seducing sighs,
They are ravished by the chimes
Of his silver-sounding rhymes,
And though man be unapproving,
Every maid is sweet and loving;
Poor, rich Poet, all his share
Of gold is in his Lady's hair;
All his diamonds, stars that rise
In the evening of her eyes;
Cold and bare,---his garret gleams
With the lightning of his dreams,
Dreams, dispelling fear and doubt,
Dreams that drive the hunger out;
Though Fate oft may overwhelm,
King is he of Fancy's realm.

LINES

It's very, very queer the way
They call this, Night, and that, the Day,
And then to parcel off the space,
And give each Week a little place.

And then reduce to months and years,
Our sorrows, blisses, hopes and fears;
'Tis very, very strange to me,
That such a foolish thing should be.

My calendar and clock shall go,
I want no dates of joy or woe,
The dawn and dusk together blend,
And stars shine out until the end.

And this is all; life is so sweet,
So grand, so glorious and complete,
So wrought of love and ecstasy,---
No man shall name my things for me.

SONG

I like no book whose hero goes
Page after page through desert prose,
And wanders wearily along,
Far from the happy hills of song.

For me a heroine who trips
With lilting lyrics on her lips,
And lovelight in her eyes sublime,
By rippling rivulets of rhyme.

ELDORADO

The yellow thirst that maddens men,
Doth lead them over bog and fen,
Through sullen seas to climes of cold,
Where wait the fertile fields of gold.

O life, O love, O hope, O fate,
Unceasing ever, early, late,
We see in dreams, by night, by day,
Some Eldorado---far away.

THE CAPTAIN

What did the noble captain do,
    Facing the death and dark,
So many souls in jeopardy
    On his beloved bark?

What did the fearless captain say,
    Or e'er he knew the worst?
"The women and the children,"
    Was his order first.

Did he look up and calmly pray,
    Facing the dark and din,
"God, let me die a thousand deaths,
    But moor my vessel in"?

SONG

If thou art not kind,
What will profit thee
Wealth of purse or mind?
If thou art not kind?
Grief and misery
Must thy portion be,
If, alas! thy heart be blind
And, poor wight, thou art not kind.

Kindness, and the earth is bright,
Kindness, and the load is light,
Kindness, and the weary way
Laughs with love and roundelay;
King is he in all his blood
Who is first in doing good;
God pity him whose heart is blind
And, alas! who is not kind.

AT LETHE WHARF

At Lethe wharf, what fleets of rhymes,
And books and tomes of bygone times,
Forgotten crafts of many climes,
    At Lethe wharf.

A thousand Poets dreamed of bliss,
A thousand Poets felt the kiss,
That Fame would press upon the brow,
But where the silent squadron now?

Close to a dismal sunken pier,
Blown by the winds of fate and fear,
They ride the tide from year to year,
    At Lethe wharf.

A PRAYER

Dear God! these narrow, mouthing fools,
    Who mewling prate their puny creeds---
These babes from theologic schools,
    Who tell a throbbing world its needs.

The howl and whine of Greek and Jew,
    Of fiends below and saints above;
They rave a thousand tirades through
    Without a syllable of Love.

But creed, and creed, and creed, and creed,
    That stifles heart, and soul, and mind;
Out of Thy goodness and their need,
    Teach them the gospel of the kind.

The myriad races mercy sue,
    But here and there a solemn clown,
Claims heaven only for the few
    Within his little tribe and town.

Dear God! Dear God! in Thy vast grace,
    Who art the Father of the Host,
Shall these blind zealots see Thy face,---
    And countless loving billions lost?

LINES AT SEA

These are the laughing waves,
    This is the happy sea,
Below are the coral caves,
    And all is mystery.

Out of the dust we came,
    Unto the dust we flee,
Weak, impotent, and lame,
    O man, thou mystery!

THE POET

He dwells apart, the birds and bees
Tell him their sweetest mysteries;
From nature, tender, good, and true,
He garners wisdom's honey-dew.

The sky, the mountain, and the mead
Are precious books where he may read,
Writ in the sunshine, on the sod,
The word, the thought, the love of God.

DREAM KISSES

I slept, I dreamed I held her close,
    And lavished kisses on her mouth,
Free as the lover wind bestows
    On maiden meadows in the south.

I slept, I dreamed, I waked to woe,
    O dawn, O dark, O vast eclipse!
I waked my lonely state to know,
    Her moist dream kisses on my lips.

MOODS

To-day my heart is warm as wine,
    And riotous with bliss;
To-day within this soul of mine
    The sweetheart fancies kiss.

And yesterday from early dawn,
    At every coward breath,
A thousand demons urged me on
    To some impending death.

REVENGE

With burning brain and heart of hate,
I sought my wronger, early, late,
And all the wretched night and day
My dream and thought was slay, and slay.

My better self rose uppermost,
The beast within my bosom lost
Itself in love; peace from afar
Shone o'er me radiant like a star.

I slew my wronger with a deed,
A deed of love; I made him bleed
With kindnesses, I filled for years
His soul with tenderness and tears.

A DEED

He did a deed, a gracious deed---
He ministered to men in need;
He bound a wound, he spoke a word
That God and every angel heard.

He did a deed, a loving deed---
Oh, souls that suffer and that bleed,
He did a deed, and on his way
A bird sang in his heart all day.

114

A GLASS OF TOKAY

In land afar 'neath Autumn skies
Some singing girl with love-lit eyes,
Pluck'd from the heavy hanging vine
The grapes that held this golden wine.

And I to-day, in after years,
Telling a truce to haunting fears,
Hold the warm beaker to my lips---
And kiss her blushing finger-tips.

Her happy laugh and careless song
This mellow tide has cherished long,
And drinking deep, methinks her voice
From out its depths bids me rejoice.

And what would soothe thy cares and mine
Sooner, O friend, than such rare wine,
Whose magic mirror holds in thrall,
Maid, music, autumn skies, and all.

IDENTITY

Tell me, after life,
    What shall be;
Tell me, after strife,
    Of death's mystery?

For weal or for woe,
    Beyond the sky,
God, let me know
    That I am I.

SONG

A sunshine heart,
   And a soul of song,
Love for hate,
   And right for wrong;
Softly speak to the weak,
   Help them along,
A sunshine heart,
   And a soul of song.

A sunshine heart,
   And a soul of song,
What though about thee
   Foemen throng?
All the day, on thy way,
   Be thou strong;
A sunshine heart,
   And a soul of song.

THE POET'S HERITAGE

Some men have wealth and vast estates,
And acres broad and palace gates,
One is a prince and one a king,
And one an humble underling.

And lo! the poet, what hath he,
That he doth trudge so merrily?
About his happy footsteps throng
A thousand little waifs of song.

LINES

My office is on land and sea,
The hours, all eternity;
I get a message from the rill,
I send a letter to the hill,
And come an Alp or Apennine,
I claim him bosom friend of mine;
For very many years I've known,
The Arctic Belt, the Torrid Zone.

The forests, lakes, the mountains, streams,
I've seen them all---in dreams, in dreams;
I listen, and they whisper me
Of Light, of Life,---Infinity;
The gulfs below, the stars above,
Come crying, "Love, and Love, and Love;"
Some morning when the compass veers,
I hope to meet some other spheres.

THE NEW BOY

Here's a health unto the boy,
He's a jewel and a joy!
Bless his little footsy feet,
Ain't he cute, and ain't he sweet?

See him fold his tiny fists,
Creased and wrinkled at the wrists,
Hear him crow, and hear him coo,
Baby, here's a health to you!

Father's happy, Mother's glad,
Blessings on the little lad!
Eyes of dawn, and tears of dew,
Baby, here's a health to you!

LAST NIGHT

Last night I sojourned for a season brief
   In goodly company; Hamlet the Dane
    Was there, and sweet Ophelia once again
Wept while she sang, her being rent with grief;
Othello came with Desdemona ere
   Iago's poison rankled in his heart;
    Orlando, swearing death should never part
His soul from fairest Rosalind's, drew near;
    And then while mirth and revel reigned supreme,
And all my soul was glad, I oped my eyes
    And marveled much that this was all a dream,
And my dear vision vanished to the skies;
   I waked to see my phantom friends no more,
   My Shakespeare lying closed upon the floor.

SONNET

Last night mad devils from an hundred hells
Ran shrieking through my racked and fevered brain,
My parched, enfeebled body throbbed with pain,
And wild eyes leered at me from dungeon cells;
The sky hung starless, and the earth lay dead,
A gulf beneath me, and the dark o'erhead;
Then a soft voice, sweeter than chiming bells,
Soothed every harsh, discordant note of woe,
And from green meadows, and from fragrant dells,
I felt again the cooling breeze blow;
The tempest in my soul became calm,
Gone all the anguish and the terror now,
For bending o'er me with her breath of balm,
My dear Love sat, her hand upon my brow.

LINES

I am no politician,
    I do not understand,
But I could be Ambassador,
    I'd go to Nature land;
Be friendly with the Forests,
    And any ragged tree,
Or lonely rock, could tell its woes
    With confidence to me.

Make treaties with the sunsets,
    The flowers, birds, and bees,
With raging, frantic oceans,
    And smiling, happy seas;
No rare acute diplomacy
    Is necessary here,
One only needs to love them much,
    And hold them very dear.

VOICES

There are voices in the air crying, "Come,"
They stir me like the magic of a drum,
On the land and on the sea,
O my soul, let us be free,
Voices, voices, ever calling to me, "Come."

There are voices in the air crying, "Come,"
O the sealèd eyes, and lips that are dumb,
Just to dream beneath the sky,
Just to live, and love, and die,
And the voices, O the voices, crying, "Come."

MARIANNA ALCAFORADO
(Love-Letters of Portuguese Nun)

Betrayed, deserted, torn with Love,
    Alas, poor Nun of Beja,
He was a wolf, and thou a dove,
    Sweet trusting Nun of Beja;
Into thy convent cote he came,
He brought thee bliss, despair and shame,
And death,---and everlasting fame,
    Dear love-lorn Nun of Beja.

When life's mad, burning day was done,
    Sad, hopeless Nun of Beja,
Didst thou, beyond the stars and sun,
    Triumphant Nun of Beja,---
Thou who didst all thy soul resign,---
Find that the highest bliss was thine,
Immortal through thy love divine,
    Undying Nun of Beja?

THE MYSTERY

I pray thee, Lord God, answer me,
Thou madest man, and what is he?
And if his soul survive the clay,
And cometh then, or night, or day?

I pray thee, Lord God, answer me,
Behind, before, are mystery;
And if man's spirit wings away,
And cometh then, or night, or day?

THIS COAT OF CLAY

This coat of clay doth hinder me,
I should away, I would be free,
This fickle flesh doth hold me here,
Betwixt a rapture and a fear.

O, brave new battles to be won,
Beyond the summit of the sun!
I should away, I would be free,
This happy dust detaineth me.

WAVES

The waves have a merry day,
When the sun and sea are gay,
Laughing, leaping, climbing, clinging,
Dancing, creeping, soaring, singing,
Now they lift their silver lips,
And their rain-bow tinted tips;
Merry, merry is the day,
When the ocean is at play.

The waves have a dreary night,
With the ocean in affright,
Running, raving, seething, scowling,
Frothing, foaming, hissing, howling,
Then beneath the tempest's breath,
Ships and men go down to death;
Dreary, dreary is the night,
With the ocean in affright.

LINES

If thou art in a grievous mood,
Seek out some sylvan solitude,
Tell all thy hearted woes and ills,
Unto the sympathetic hills,
Or the sea, and hear her voice,
Bidding thee conquer and rejoice;
The mountain, valley, and the glen
Will lead thee to thyself again,
Will soothe thy sorrow, right thy wrong,
And kiss thy lips to sweetest song;
O trust in Nature, love but her,
The best, the wisest comforter.

SONG

I heard a bird flood all the night
With strains of rapture and delight,
The leaves leaned low to listen, and
The sleepy trees could understand.

Many the birds---and folk by day,
Sing when the golden world is gay,
But, O my heart, the men who might,
Who bravely sing through sorrow's night!

TO ELIZABETH

Elizabeth, Elizabeth,
Thy lips might lure a man to death,
Thy face, thy form, thy bosom's swell,
Might tempt a man to happy hell.

And yet if for some grace of thine,
He should his soul to woe resign,
Thy sweet eyes with tearful rain,
Would lead him heavenward again.

THIS WOULD BE A BLESSED DAY

This would be a blessed day,
If a verse would pass my way,
If a rose-leaf rhyme would drip
All its dew upon my lip,
Come in tender, loving guise,
Make a river of mine eyes,
Circle in the air and rest
In the bastion of my breast.

Muse, dear Muse, O bring to me
One deep draught of Poetry,
I am thinking and I long
For a flagon full of song,
Muse, dear Muse, without thine art
Midnight hovers o'er my heart,
Hell were heaven with thee, and
Without thee, earth is arid land.

This would be a blessed day,
If a verse would pass my way.

WRATH AND LOVE

Wrath is a wrinkled hag, hell-born,
Her heart is hate, her soul is scorn,
Blinded with blood, she can not see
To do a deed of charity.

Love is a maiden young and fair,
She kissed the brow of dumb despair
Till comfort came; ah, love is she,
Whose other name is Charity.

SONG

A knitter in the sun is one
Who weaves the tangled threads of thought
Into a perfect robe of rhyme,
Who blends the multi-colored words
To one harmonious whole;
And then if he hath wisely wrought,
And garnered in the fields of thyme,
Hath caught the carol of the birds
To echo ever in his soul,---
O joy unspeakable for one,
Who is a knitter in the sun.

LINES

Poet, Poet, enter in,
Guiltless be thy soul of sin,
A double blessing on thy brow,
Holy is the moment now.

Poet, this should be to thee,
The sweetest sanctuary,
Rarest day twixt life and death,
When mind of man travaileth.

Poet, Poet, enter in,
Follow faithful, thou shalt win,
God hath sworn to give to thee
Deathless immortality.

Poet, in thy days of youth,
Banish error, worship truth,
When thou art infirm and old,
Happiness shall thee enfold.

Poet, Poet, enter in,
Thou art priest and paladin,
Who hath fear of hell or death,
When mind of man travaileth?

ALL ATONING END

I am so overwhelmed with shame,
    For evil I have done,
I hate the sound of my vile name,
    O weak, unworthy son!

O'erwhelmed with grief and shame am I,
    Dear God, I pray Thee send
Me some white deed in which to die,
    An all atoning end.

IN PINK AND WHITE

In pink and white the orchards lie,
Fragrant beneath an April sky,
The golden summer draweth nigh,
      In pink and white.

A robin in an apple-tree,
In carolling ecstasy---
And O puissant heart of me,

That little recks of fate or fear,
For Preciosa's cheek is near
Where blushes blossom all the year
      In pink and white.

THE POET'S SOUL

Within his soul are singing birds
And diamond thoughts and golden words,
Mountains, meadows, lowing herds,
    Within his soul;

And joy and sorrow, darkness, light,
Sunshine and shadow, day and night,
Hatred of wrong and love of right;

And one eternal, constant prayer,
A hunger and a thirst are there,
For deathless deeds to do, to dare---
    Within his soul.

LEPERS

"Unclean! Unclean!" the wretched lepers cry,
"Unclean! Unclean! O mortal, come not nigh,
Nor touch our garments, lest the dread disease
Doom thee to death and untold agonies."

And thou and I, base moral lepers, vile,
Who greet the righteous with a conscious smile,
We deem our grainèd spots unknown, unseen,
Thou, thou, and I, should stand and cry, "Unclean!"

SONG

The valiant sun leaps up the east,
    Soul of myself be strong!
Death is the dessert to life's feast,
    Soul of myself be strong!
Over the arching, lucent sky
Gay cloud craft are sailing by,
We love, we weep, we dream, we die,
    Soul of myself be strong!

Youth is hasty, age is slow,
    Soul of myself be strong!
Into the night we groping go,
    Soul of myself be strong!
After the darkness cometh light,
Wrong shall captive be to right,
Mine eye is fixèd on the height,
    Soul of myself be strong!

NOT WITH FEAR

The poet hath no fear of death,
    Nor any fear of life;
The poet with his honey breath
    Doth drown the strains of strife;
And only when his muse is near
The poet trembles---not with fear.

The poet hath no fear of man,
    Nor any fear of hell;
His soldier-soul doth boldly plan
    To conquer, to excel;
But when his worshipped muse is near
The poet trembles---not with fear.

SONG

My lyric pen is palsied when
Some sin is heavy on my soul,
When conscience, dun as murky night,
Rebels against my wrong of right,
Proclaims me traitor in the fight,
And all unworthy of the goal,
Some demon daunts my lyric pen.

My lyric pen is swiftest when
A light illumineth my heart,
Some sense serene of duty done,
Some noble enterprise begun,
A foe forgive, battle won;
Oh, then with an immortal art
An angel speeds my lyric pen.

FROM DEVONSHIRE

From Devonshire these roses came,
With souls of sweetness, hearts of flame,
They bear a message mute frae hame,
      From Devonshire.

To thee each petal must recall,
Some memory that doth enthrall,
Of England, blown across her wall;

To me---they mirror in my mind,
Warm with the wooing of the wind,
Another rose---of womankind,
      From Devonshire.

TREES

The trees within the wood,
Are patient, wise, and good,
The light the forest aisles
In the summer with their smiles,
And in winter-time they know
All the glory of the snow;
Every bird may build and brood,
In the trees within the wood.

The trees within the wood,
Are much misunderstood,
They are beautiful and kind
To the fickle-minded wind;
They are fondly gazed upon
By the yellow, mellow sun;
There is fuel, there is food,
In the trees within the wood.

The trees within the wood
Are of every hue and mood,
Some are solemn, some are gay,
Some prefer the night to day;
When I transmigrate I'll be
Just a mighty monarch tree,
Lofty, and of royal blood,
Growing great within the wood.

GRIEF

Grief came by and beckoned me,
  (Pity my bleeding eyes,)
I was buoyant, young, and free,
  Now I am wounds and sighs;
Grief called out "O, Ho! O, Ho!
What dost thou know to tell of woe?
Let me but clutch thee;" so, and so;---
  (Pity my sunken eyes.)

Grief on me hath set his seal,
  (Pity my poor dim eyes,)
These old wounds so slowly heal,
  In days of youth be wise;
Here, pale Sorrow, face me fair,
I'll fight thy legions of despair,
Until no enemy is there,
  Despite my sightless eyes.

TO THEE

At first, at last, at birth, at death,
    We come to Thee,
Still let us with our latest breath,
    Sing praises to Thee:
By day, by night, through storm and calm,
    We come to Thee.
O let our life be one sweet psalm,
    To Thee, to Thee.

Father, when pain and anguish are,
    We come to Thee,
A good deed shineth like a star,
    To Thee, to Thee,
Over the narrow span of years,
    We come to Thee,
After the sorrow and the tears,
    To Thee, to Thee.

Our souls have known the dark travail,
    We come to Thee,
Sun, moon, and stars, their faces pale,
    To Thee, to Thee,
Dear God, the journey's end is near,
    We come to Thee,
In faith and love, without a fear,
    To Thee, to Thee.

THE END.

The
Gates
of Silence

with

Interludes of Song

Originally published in 1903

INDEX TO FIRST LINES

I

The races rise and fall,
   The nations come and go,
Time tenderly doth cover all
   With violets and snow.

The mortal tide moves on
   To some immortal shore,
Past purple peaks of dusk and dawn,
   Into the evermore.

II

I could not see till I was blind,
   Then color, music, light,
Came floating down on every wind
   And noonday was at night.

I could not feel till I was dead;
   Then through the mold and wet
A rose breathed softly overhead,
   I heard a violet.

III

One by one, the gods we know
    Weary of our trust,
One by one, the prophets go
    Dreaming to the dust.

All the cobweb creeds of men
    Vanish into air,
Leaving nothing, save a "When?"
    Nothing, save a "Where?"

IV

From the dim starry track
Never a man comes back;
Of future weal or woe
Never a man doth know.

Nor you, nor I, nor he,
Can solve the mystery;
Come, let us boldly press
On to the fathomless.

V

All the tomes of all the tribes,
All the songs of all the scribes,
All that priest and prophet say,
What is it? and what are they?

Fancies futile, feeble, vain,
Idle dream-drift of the brain,---
As of old the mystery
Doth encompass you and me.

SONG

It isn't raining rain to me,
   It's raining daffodils;
In every dimpled drop I see
   Wild flowers on the hills;
The clouds of gray engulf the day,
   And overwhelm the town;
It isn't raining rain to me,
   It's raining roses down.

It isn't raining rain to me,
   But fields of clover bloom,
Where every buccaneering bee
   May find a bed and room!
A health unto the happy!
   A fig for him who frets!---
It isn't raining rain to me,
   It's raining violets.

VI

Old and yet young, the jocund Earth
    Doth speed among the spheres,
Her children of imperial birth
    Are all the golden years.

The happy orb sweeps on,
    Led by some vague unrest,
Some mystic hint of joys unborn,
    Springing within her breast.

VII

What if I wake in the dark
    After the last long sleep?
What if no friendly spark
    Vigil about me keep?

What if the alien shores
    Baffle my blinded barque,
And lost on some wild Azores,---
    What if I wake in the dark?

VIII

So much I love God's sky,
    And all He giveth me,
That when I come to die,
    I feel how it will be.

My swift soul as it flies
    In triumphant singing on,
Will pass still lakes of Moonrise,
    And wild cataracts of Dawn.

IX

Poor rambling, shambling soul of mine,
    Beyond the night, beyond the day,
When thou dost unto death resign
    This happy habitat of clay,

In high conclave, at feasts divine,
    Will legions leap to heed thy nod?
Or, doomed to darkness, wilt thou whine,
    A beggar at the gates of God?

X

What of the men of Mars,
    And maids of Mercury?
What of the loves and wars
    These swirling systems see?

How do the Moon-folk fare?
    What ships ply Saturn's seas?
And what brave races rare
    Throng the proud Pleiades?

SONG

The Dawn is a wild, fair woman,
    With sunrise in her hair;
Look where she stands, with pleading hands,
    To lure me there.

The Dusk is dark and glorious,
    A star upon her brow;
With sunset blushes in her cheeks,
    She beckons now.

I, ever fickle, stand between,
    Upon my lips a rune,
And in my summer-singing soul---
    The hoiden happy Noon.

XI

I want no trickster God,---
   No cunning, crafty spook---
Who smites a people, or a rock,
   Or one who writes a book.

For me a God who flings
   Out of his spendthrift hands
The whirling worlds like pebbles,
   The meshèd stars like sand.

XII

I sought the sun,---he struggled on;
   The moon made no reply,
I questioned every nomad star
   Upon the desert sky.

But never syllable or sign
   To my impatient breath,---
Give me the plummet, Pilot;
   I will sound the deeps of death.

XIII

I know not what it is,
   I know not where nor how,
But while the pallid kiss
   Of Death is on my brow.

My dauntless soul will leap
   In eager quest to find
Where God doth love and keep
   His flocks of humankind.

XIV

Where are the legioned dead
   Of all the pallid past?
Out of the flesh they sped,
   On to the unknown vast.

Tented upon the air?
   By valiant spirits led?
How and when, ---and where,---
   Where are the legioned dead?

XV

The Earth's a burly animal
   With fearless man astride;
Down the rugged gulfs of time,
   He doth boldly ride.

The Earth's a burly animal
   Bellowing through space,
Bearing upon his shaggy back---
   And where---man's royal race?

SONG

Here are roses for a rose,
　　Fragrance for the fair,
For thy soft noontide bosom
　　And thy twilight hair.

Let each pleading petal tell
　　All my passion's woe;
Crush my crimson couriers
　　To thy heart of snow.

Crush them with thy sweet kisses
　　Down to drowsy death,
Make their pure souls immortal
　　With thy holy breath.

XVI

When Fate hath dealt his mortal thrust,
   And love and life are gone,
The body will dissolve to dust,---
   The gaunt soul stagger on

Across vast continents of space,
   And shoreless seas of air,
Seeking its new appointed place,
   Again to do, to dare.

XVII

The body is the barque
   That bears the soul away,
Down to the docks of dark,
   Down to the harbor gray.

Then suddenly along,
   The spirit leaps afar,
On, on, from zone to zone,
   On, on, from star to star.

XVIII

What new visions we shall see
    With immortal eyes?
What vast pageants will there be
    Passing in the skies?

What new melodies shall greet
    Our immortal ears,
When we reach the far retreat
    O'er the bridge of years?

XIX

The earth doth bravely swing about
    The hills and vales of space,
In God's sweet coronal of worlds,
    It keeps its joyous pace.

Flung from the hand Omnipotent,
    Until old Time be gray
The vaulted Night will hoard her stars,
    The Sun will drink the day.

XX

What shall be when we are free
  Of all earthen care?
What do our pale brethren see
  In the otherwhere?

Is it noon, or is it night,
  T' other side of death?
Pilot! is a land of light
  Just beyond our breath?

SONG

Back to the siren South,
  Each mad red rose aglow,
To the vintage of her mouth,
  Where purple kisses grow.

Back to her Orient eyes,
  Her bosom's buds ablow;
Languorous land of ardent skies,
  What should the cold North know?

XXI

It is a daring flight
    That doth await the soul,
Across an unknown night
    Unto an unknown goal.

Beyond the gates of space,
    Away, and yet away,
To find the ordained place,
    Upon the destined day.

XXII

What is it, where is it,---how is it
    After the day is done?
What goal and fate for love and hate,
    Beyond the lusty sun?

How is it, where is it,---what is it
    Nirvana, heaven, hell?
Shakespeare, Omar, Solomon,
    Will not God let you tell?

163

XXIII

My mind is fast made up,---
    If God doth thwart me here,
I'll seek on somewhere east of Mars,
    Or west of Jupiter.

I will not be denied,
    My eager soul must know
And find my brethren who have died
    Through all the long ago.

XXIV

The hills about my village throng
    With steadfast friends of mine;
They stand up brave, and tall, and strong,
    Sir Oak, Sir Elm, Sir Pine.

Subjects of sun, and wind, and sky,
    They wait, they wave, they pray.
Alas, alas! that you and I
    Cannot be calm as they!

XXV

It is not fair that God should keep
    The secret to His breast,
And drift us down to dreamless sleep,
    The mystery unguessed.

No voice from out the silence calls,
    No finger points the way,---
Blind beggars shut between the walls,---
    The walls of night and day.

SONG

Folly, we, alas! have been
Jocund, oft and time again;
Modest Virtue now shall be
Fair handmaiden unto me.

In thy loving eyes the tears
Hallowed half the wastrel years;
Ocean odors in thy hair,
Lips that led to Passion's lair.

Farewell, Folly, let us part,
Bind the old wounds in the heart;
Gentle Virtue now shall be
Sweet handmaiden unto me.

XXVI

Life, thou art so beautiful,
  Cheek and eyes and hair,
God doth seem to think and dream,
  How to make thee fair.

And thy swarthy sister,
  With her hooded brow
And her muffled lips of lead;---
  What, O Death, art thou?

XXVII

Out beyond the bourn of things,
Where each star a censer swings,
Infant orbs are taking flight
From the teeming womb of Night.

And o'er vasty voids of space,
Reeling on from place to place,
Worn and wrinkled, gaunt and gray,
Worlds are tott'ring to decay.

XXVII

Who hath known, and who hath seen,
   And who can testify?
What bold adventurer hath been
   To star-lands in the sky?

Books there be, for you and me,
   Maps of the charted "Whence;"
Alas, my sceptic soul must see
   Some better evidence.

XXIX

I went in search of Beauty,
   Up and down, and far and wide
And streaming, beaming, gleaming
   She was ever at my side.

I went in search of Beauty,
   Over meadow, over mart,
And leaping, creeping, weeping,
   She was ever in my heart.

XXX

Morn leaps in mailèd gold,
    And cries, "Lo, I am Youth,
O daring deed, and bold,
    I covet honor, truth."

Night clasps her patient stars
    Close to her loving breast,
And, proud of life's brave scars,
    Says softly, "I must rest."

SONG

I humbly thank the gods benign,
For all the blessings that are mine.

My books, my garden, and my dog,
For mountain, meadow, fen, and bog.

The morning drips her dew for me,
Noon spreads an opal canopy.

Home-bound, the drifting cloud-crafts rest
Where sunset ambers all the west;

Soft o'er the poppy fields of sleep
The drowsy winds of dreamland creep.

What idle things are wealth and fame
Beside the treasures one could name!

I humbly thank the gods benign,
For all the blessings that are mine.

XXXI

We are captives close confined
    To this cockle-shell of clay;
Let us horse the champing wind,
    Let us stride to worlds away.

Let us sail the seas of space,
    To celestial affairs afar,
And go voyaging apace,
    On from peopled star to star.

XXXII

Why is my wretched body old?
    My heart is young and free;
My soul, undaunted, wild, and bold,
    Doth leap in ecstasy.

Yet Time doth clutch me at the throat,
    And wields his potent sway,
Dumb Charon waiteth by the boat,---
    We must away, away.

XXXIII

O for the centuries to be,
Of beauty and simplicity,
When wisdom, love, and truth shall reign,
And science slay disease and pain.

When all the nations shall be blent
Into one loving parliament,
When wars are done, and earth shall be
One peaceful, happy family.

XXXIV

After a million years
    Have stored their wealth away,
What will our finer kinsmen think
    Of us who live to-day?

Will some say, " 'T is a jest;
    They had not souls at all"?
And other, "Never say that we
    Sprang from such animal"?

XXXV

What of the instant when
   The soul fares forth the clay?
What might moment then
   Of rapture or dismay?

What have the gods in store,
   What vast, auspicious scheme,
Behind death's darkened door,---
   Beyond our wildest dream?

SONG

Love distilleth in thine eyes,
   Such a draught divine,
That I am not overwise,
   Draining down the wine.

For with reeling soul afire,
   Staggering 'mong men,
I am frenzied with desire---
   But to drink again.

XXXVI

That old red fear comes over me,
   The stealthy haunting dread,
That when the sod doth cover me
   My soul, too, shall be dead.

Why think the soul survives its clay,
   Even an instant's span?
What beacon holds aloft a ray,
   Presumptuous proud man?

XXXVII

What star-shod paths lead up to God
   We may not know, we may not see;
The highways that the dead have trod
   Are curtained close with mystery.

But if this goodly earth and fair
   Be token of infinite grace,
Ah, who can dream the glories rare
   In store for man's immortal race!

XXXVIII

When death should smooth my furrowed face
    And still my breathèd woes,
I thought to come unto that place
    Of rapture and repose.

At last my free soul outward sped
    Unto the destined sphere;
"We wonder," there the spirits said,
    "Where we shall go from here."

XXXIX

Notwithstanding all that's writ,
    Nothing, nothing, do we know,
Mystery doth encompass it
    Till the soul doth further go.

All the guesses idle are,
    All the prophecies are vain;
Death may solve the riddle rare,---
    This is but a guess again.

XL

I waked from out the drowse of death
    That held my spirit fast;---
"Sleep on," a soft voice said, and yet
    A billion years had passed.

The tireless æons onward sped
    Until a golden chime
Rang from the dark; the voice then said,
    "Rouse thee, 't is now thy time."

XLI

In vain, in vain,---we may not know
    God's secret wise and true,
Down to the doors of death we go
    And pass the portals through.

What silly heavens in the skies
    The prating prophets plan!
Some unimagined, vast surprise
    Shall greet the soul of man!

XLII

O mystery of mysteries,
　　O secret vast and rare,
We stretch blind hands unto the skies,
　　We fathom everywhere.

From the dumb silence comes no sound,
　　No syllable we hear,
And man must venture outward bound,
　　A chartless voyager.

XLIII

Why one poor heaven?---there may be
　　A thousand after this;
The soul, from fleshy fetters free,
　　May climb from bliss to bliss.

From high and then to higher still,
　　And nobler battles won,
Guided by God's omniscient will,
　　Go on, and on, and on.

XLIV

Who is Infinity---
  Who governeth all things---
How sweet to Him must be
  Our simple offerings!

The incense of our deeds,
  The fragrance of our faith,
While on the chariot speeds---
  To destination Death.

XLV

After the day, the night,
  After the month, the year,---
Naught will survive the dark and light
  Save Pity's melting tear.

After the life, and death,---
  How swift the moments speed!
Naught will survive our fleeting breath
  Save kindly word and deed.

SONG

Come to my ears, come to my heart,
 Laugh from my lips, O Song,
Cry to me, sigh to me, hie to me, fly to me,
 Sing in my soul, O Song;
Below is the wave, and above is the sky,
 Croon to me, swoon to me, Song;
Creep to me, weep to me, laggard, O leap to me,---
 Let us away from wrong.

Stay with me, pray with me, Song, O away with me,
 Far let us venture afar,
Over the deep to a still harbor bar,
 "Neath some sweet, penitent star;
O tender haze of the heart's happy days,
 O the fond fancies that throng!
A truce unto care and isles of despair,
 Haste to my heart, O Song!

XLVI

All else of Man is dead, and I
    Stand lone upon the sphere;
The pale earth shivers, sigh on sigh,
    And shakes with frenzied fear.

Some Titan tears the world apart,
    And sets the seas to rout,
And I, a silence at my heart,
    See the cold sun fade out.

XLVII

Another day comes up the east,
    And totters down the west;
Another night will rock to sleep
    The stars upon her breast.

Year in, year out, they file along,
    Sans intermission thus,---
I sometimes think the program is
    A bit monotonous.

XLVIII

Over the sea we go,---
   Over the sea of life,
Past reefs of want and woe,
   Through blinding fogs of strife.

O happy sea and wind,---
   Soon, soon, we will forget
The islands far behind,
   Those islands of regret.

XLIX

I weep so often now,
   It may be death is near;
A calm is on my brow,
   A song within mine ear.

I weep so often now---
   Come, faith and love and trust,
And teach me humbly how
   The valiant go to dust.

L

I do not grieve my soul
    Concerning what will be
While Time's broad billows roll
    On to Eternity.

I know the dawns of days
    That drink the darkness there
Will blossom into gorgeous Noons,
    Up-pilèd everywhere.

SONG

What care I for caste or creed?
It is the deed, it is the deed;
What for class or what for clan?
It is the man, it is the man;
Heirs of love, and joy, and woe,
Who is high, and who is low?
Mountain, valley, sky, and sea,
Are for all humanity.

What care I for robe or stole?
It is the soul, it is the soul;
What for crown, or what for crest?
It is the heart within the breast;
It is the faith, it is the hope,
It is the struggle up the slope,
It is the brain and eye to see,
One God, and one humanity.

THE END.

Songs from a Georgia Garden

and

Echoes from
The Gates of Silence

Originally published in 1904

Under the greenwood tree,
Who loves to lie with me;---

. . . .

Come hither, come hither, come hither.

Amiens Song.

CONTENTS
SONGS FROM A GEORGIA GARDEN

THE GATES OF SILENCE

I

Because I never cared for fame,
    Fame came and cared for me;
I who had sent her soul to shame,
    And hell, and infamy.

Because I never cared for fame,
    Fame came and cared for me;
God-glowing now with hearts aflame,
    We brook our ecstasy.

II

To-morrow will be another day,
    Let this grim one go
Steep'd to his starven soul in shame,
    Fat with his paunch of woe.

To-morrow will be another day,
    God! how the sun burns bright;
Phaethon! thou fool, the chariot,
    Come! usher in the Night!

III

I thought to cull thee roses,
　　But bear a sprig of rue
Pain-purpled in its closes,
　　Both bitter-sweet and true.

I thought to cull thee roses,
　　Take now thy wreath of me,
Hang it on thy bruisèd heart,
　　I gathered it for thee.

IV

My Muse is like a woman; she
Doth trouble, tease, and torture me,
Then in a moment sobs and clings
About me with soft murmurings.

My Muse is like a woman; she
Doth woo me with her witchery---
By Hecate, and the hosts of hell,
I love no woman half so well!

V
MY HEART AND MY SOUL AND I

The sun, and the sea, and the wind,
    The wave, and the wind, and the sky,
We are off to a magical Ind,
    My heart, and my soul, and I;
Behind us the isles of despair
    And mountains of misery lie.
We're away, anywhere, anywhere,
    My heart, and my soul, and I.

O islands and mountains of youth,
    O land that lies gleaming before,
Life is love, hope, and beauty, and truth,---
    We will weep o'er the past no more.
Behind, are the bleak fallow years,
    Before, are the sea and the sky,
We're away, with a truce to the tears,
    My heart, and my soul, and I.

VI

I know why thou wast born my song,
  I know thy wild sweet ecstasy,
I know why all thy soul doth throng
  With passion, tears, and melody.

'Tis that my Lady loveth thee,
  And from her lips thou seen wilt flow,
Singing with tender sympathy,
  Of all our bliss, of all our woe.

VII

A flake at a time the dawn drifts down,
  Filling the world with light;
Heart of my heart, in dreams of thee
  I smiled away the night.

And now 'tis morn, the garish sun
  Doth flaunt his lurid beams;
Speed day, speed light; come quickly, night,
  Bringing again my dreams.

VIII

The deep dusk drifted down,
  A star dreamed in the sky,
Heart to fond heart alone
  We were, my bride and I.

At dawn a wisp of light
  Came flick'ring faint and fair,
To kiss her bosom's white,
  Her lips, her eyes, her hair.

IX

Here is my Lady Butterfly,
  And there is Baron Bee,
Sir Humming-bird is preening nigh
  Upon a cedar-tree.

These royal folk are very gay,
  For bud and bush and bloom,
All know, Queen Rose at noon to-day
  Doth hold her Drawing Room.

X
LA JACONDE

Mona Lisa, Mona Lisa,
    Did Da Vinci know?
All that smile's inscrutable
    Love, and bliss, and woe?

Mona Lisa, Mona Lisa,
    Did those pleading hands
Lead him up, and on, and out
    O'er Love's lotus lands?

Mona Lisa, Mona Lisa,
    Bless our wild, fond fears;
Love doth dwell deep down thine eyes---
    Deeper far than tears.

XI

Turiddu, thee, this woman loved,
  With all her tender, melting charms;
See how she wept, and laughed, and clung
  In the close shelter of thy arms.

Turiddu, now the woman hates,
  Silent the wood-dove's cooing note,
Look, lest in blinded fury she
  Shall leap and clutch thy tawny throat.

XII

I pinèd in a palace grand,
Amid the fruits of Samarcand,
The fountains murmured wearily,---
My dear Muse had forsaken me.

Confinèd in a dungeon I
Reveled in dreams of ecstasy;---
By day, by night, within my soul,
My Muse sang like an oriole.

XIII

I caught a noontide hour
    Fast eager in my hand;
I held it like a flower
    I sought to understand.

I pluck'd its petals softly
    Of moments each away;
I long'd to learn the thoughts that burn
    The bosom of the day.

XIV

Take these timid violets,
    Weeping with the dew;
Shy as tricksy triolets,
    All for you, for you.

To your bosom hold them,
    Whispering my cares;
In your heart enfold them,
    Heed their purple prayers.

XV
SONG

Valerie is very young,---
    Valerie is very fair,
Past the telling of the tongue,
    Is the glory of her hair;
And the magic of her words
    To the music of her voice,
Ringing, singing, seem to say,
    "O thou son of man rejoice."

Valerie is very young,---
    O'er her brow in splendid rolled,
Shining strands of gold are strung,
    Titan, trembling, might behold,
And my heart and soul are caught,
    Captive, in the meshes there,
Valerie is very young,---
    Valerie is very fair.

XVI

He wantons with the blushing East,
   He woos the naked Noon,
The shameless Summer spreads a feast,
   When he doth clasp the June.

And his forsaken bride of old,
   Disdainful in distress,
Wanders o'er Night's star fields of gold,
   Cold, pale, and passionless.

XVII

This Stradivari, sweet and good,
Was wrought of mellow, fragrant wood,
Sent breathing sylvan song and stir
To Cremona's artificer.

Now Marian holds the violin
Beneath her warmly huddling chin;
Listen, and you may dreaming be
Again in love, and Italy.

XVIII

Drenched in a dew of tender tears,
   A Song doth blossom in my heart,
The trembling words are fraught with fears,
   The melody is love's sweet art.

O to my Lady, song, away,
   Be thou my courier, true and fleet,
Mesh her in music all the day,
   Then die in fragrance at her feet.

XIX

My heart was burned out long ago,
My bosom is a waste of snow,
And lonely as a pale lagoon,
In the dead mountains of the moon.

Could grim Vesuvius in an hour
Spend all his raging, potent power,
'Tis he, alone, might feebly know
How my heart burned out long ago.

XX
TEAR SONG

A merry young bush,
 And a happy old tree,
A song of a thrush,
 And a wave of the sea;
A cloud in the sky,
 And sweet tear-drops of rain,
A monarch am I,
 On a poor couch of pain.

A forest of faith
 In a valley of dreams,
"Be thou true unto death,"
 Sob the murmuring streams;
In glory the sun
 Doth relinquish his reign,
The battle is won
 On the red field of pain.

XXI

The dark is dying, dying,
　　Weary, faint, forlorn,
I fling my casement open
　　To clasp the virgin Morn.

And now the Day is dying---
　　She that I love, I swear,
But see,---th' Evening woman,
　　With star-dust in her hair.

XXII

A mist came over the mountain,
　　A mist came over the sea;
The mist rose up from the fountain,
　　Singing a song to me.

O mist of the beautiful mountain,
　　O mist of the sorrowful skies,
My heart is a deep widening fountain
　　Splashing this mist to my eyes.

XXIII

The wind is such a gossip,
    I must be very still,
For every idle word I breathe
    He'll carry o'er the hill.

And shrub, and rock, and bird, and tree,
    That I love jealously,
May form some queer opinion
    Of poor old foolish me.

XXIV

The rhymes came in the rain,
    After long sway of sun,
Weeping, singing, with love and pain,
    The rhymes came in the rain.

Up to my heart they crept,
    Deserted, torn, and slain!
We dream'd, we danc'd, we wept,
    The rhymes came in the rain.

XXV
ABELARD AND HELOISE

Abelard and Heloise,
Ne'er were lovers like to these;
Flying in the face of fate,
Ground beneath then heel of hate,
Constant to the latest breath,
With a faith defying death,
Deeper than unsounded seas,---
Abelard and Heloise.

Abelard and Heloise,
Drained Love's chalice to the lees;
Joyed and sorrowed, laughed and wept,
Tempest-torn and passion-swept;
Now they dream away the days
In the peaceful Pere la Chaise,
Sleeping there beneath the trees,---
Abelard and Heloise.

XXVI

Out of the turbid pool of Night,
　　Out of the storm and gloom,
Morn, like a lily, pure and white,
　　Blossoms within my room.

Out of our bosom's hopeless Night,
　　Out of the rack and ruth,
Perchance may spring to life and light,
　　Lilies of love and truth.

XXVII

Some time the rhyme will come and cling,
And leap, and laugh, and shout, and sing,
And whisper love, and joy, and bliss,
And coo and woo, and clasp and kiss.

Or oft the little rhyme will weep,
And in the bosom, sobbing, sleep
Glad rhymes, sad rhymes, that bubble up
Within the Poet's magic cup.

XXVIII

A certain thought hath followed me,
    A fortnight and a day,
And what I do or where I be,
    The thought will not away.

To-day, again, he came and tried
    My sympathy to win,
I think I'll ope my bosom wide
    And let the fellow in.

XXIX

You never see a bird alone,
    There are always two;
Men and women singly moan;
    Birds know how to woo.

The birds are never bachelors,
    Or spinsters all unblest,
They wisely know the happiness
    Within a sacred nest.

XXX

A ROSE IN WINTER

Tell me, I pray thee, gracious Rose,
The burden of thy wintry woes,
Why now thou seemest to despair,
Within the florist's window there.
Is it, as I have often heard,
About, you know, Sir Mocking-bird?
Or doth thy soul this sadness see,
In dreams of beetle, and of bee,
Of June, and Noon, and Summer sky,
And gossips with the butterfly,
While in some happy apple-tree
A robin sang in ecstasy?
Is this thy sorrow, this thy care,
Within the florist's window there?

XXXI

When my dear Love is absent,
   And in lonely grief I stand,
My bosom is in Egypt
   With a famine on the land.

But when she cometh to me
   With a tender, trusting smile,
By bosom is in Egypt
   With an overflowing Nile.

XXXII

A riot in the rose-bush,
   A scuffle in the grass;
The frightened flowers wonder
   If war has come to pass.

A chatter and a clatter,
   A wriggle and a squirm,
And all the row about a plump
   And juicy little worm.

XXXIII

In youth mine eager eyes were bright,
Dazzled with all joy's golden light,
Wild, ardent, with unbridled haste,
Unwisely did I see and taste.

At peace am I, calm, poor, and old,
Nor fierce for fame, or lust for gold,
Through my blind eyes I trancèd see
These truths once dim and scant to me.

XXXIV

Clad in a bridal robe of snow,
    The Jungfrau waiteth white and still,
As the slow ages come and go,
    For one to tame her haughty will.

While dull, poor centuries go by,
    Mont Blanc, the monarch, lone doth stand,
Throned high upon his Alpine sky,
    Looking to her Switzerland.

XXXV
TO HENI

Heni live, and Heni died,
    Forty-five hundred years ago,
This is his skeleton bleached and dried,
    Snug in a box in Mummy Row;
How he fought, and how he fared,
    Never a chronicle doth show,
And of the dangers that he dared,
    Forty-five hundred years ago.
Just his dry bones in a case,
    The oldest chap in Mummy Row;
Whether his thought was broad or base,
    Never a syllable I'll know;
Making the rounds I found him there,
    Careless of years that ebb and flow,
Shut from the sweet and balmy air,
    Forty-five hundred years ago.
This his fate, and this his fame,
    Children come and stand tiptoe,
People pause and read the name,
    The pioneer of Mummy Row;
By the Nilus' fruitful tide,
    Where lily and lotus grow,
Heni lived, and Heni died,
    Forty-five hundred years ago.

XXXVI
STAR SONG

Go home, Father Sun, send old Mother Moon,
    Along with the baby stars,
And we will wait at the little gate,
    Down by the meadow bars.
Hurry home, hurry home,
    Happy Father Sun, West of the meadow bars,
And send us soon, old Mother Moon,
    And all the baby stars.

Now Mother Moon is coming up the East,
    East of the meadow bars,
And twinkling after, with light and laughter,
    Follow the baby stars.
Follow your Mother Moon, happy little stars,
    Over the fields above;
Come again to-morrow night,
Bubbling over with delight,
    Little baby stars of love.

XXXVII
IN ANCIENT GREECE

In ancient Greece sweet Sappho turned
Her thoughts to words that breathed and burned,
O temples, lutes, and incense urn'd
      In ancient Greece.

Art, learning, grace, and beauty's bliss
Blossomed in the Acropolis,---
But lo, the woman, tender, true,

Who leans to me with lips of dew,
And love immortal in her eyes---
Thank God, I lived not with the wise
      In ancient Greece.

XXXVIII
IN SWITZERLAND

In Switzerland the mountains stand
Like sentinels to guard the land,
The sun doth wield a magic wand
     In Switzerland.

The lakes are gold and amethyst,
Where sky, and light, and cloud have kissed,
And up the crag, and down the dell,

On snowy height, or summer mead,
The wind doth ever whisper "Tell;"
The waters murmur "Winkelreid,"
     In Switzerland.

XXXIX

I follow Song,---
Unto the utmost East I follow Song.
Song dawns with day, it dreams with dusk,
It lights the happy stars upon their way,
It calms the wild, weird fears that throng:
I follow Song.

I follow Song.
There youth and love go laughing, hand in hand;
There sorrow, joy, and hope and tears.
Are of one gentle, weeping, sister band,
Sent to illumine man's impassioned years:
I follow Song.

I follow Song.
O Death, made dear by sweetest melody,
Come thou at noon or night, I go
Fondly to thy embrace, so thou wilt show
Unto my soul the Soul of Poetry:
I follow Song.

XL

We are so merry, contented, and gay,
    Enid and I and the baby,
What do we care for the Appian Way,
    Enid and I and the baby?
Politics, wars, and the tariff may go,
Little we reck how the fickle winds blow,
We're a triumvirate, mighty and low,
    Enid and I and the baby.

Climb up, my little son, here to my knee---
    Enid and I and the baby,
Isn't he sturdy and brave as could be?
    Enid and I and the baby;
Take him, my dear, he is weary with play,
See how he blinks in that Sleepy-town way,
Here is a kiss all around, and hurrā---
    Enid and I and the baby.

XLI
MORNING SONG

Every little blade of grass
Says "Good-Morning" when we pass;
Every tree doth nod and say,
" 'Tis a rare" or "Rainy day;"

Every rose on every bush,
Be it Brier, Moss, or Blush,
Lifts its lips in fragrant bliss
For a caress or a kiss.

Would we only list and hear
All they whisper in our ear,
Thou and I need never know
Foolish words like "Want" and "Woe;"

I and thou in tranquil ways
Might employ the nights and days;
Nature loveth to confer
Peace on him who heedeth her.

XLII
BYRON, SHELLEY, KEATS, AND POE

Byron, Shelley, Keats, and Poe,
Wrath and rapture, wit and woe;
Dreamers, debauchees divine,
Frantic with a frenzy fine,
Hearts of fire, souls of snow,
Byron, Shelley, Keats, and Poe.

Byron, Shelley, Keats, and Poe,
Oh, sweet pain the Poets know;
Doomed and damned, and crowned, and caught
To bliss upon the wings of thought;
Brain and vein, and pulse aglow,
Byron, Shelley, Keats, and Poe.

Byron, Shelley, Keats, and Poe,
Kingdoms crumble, empires go,
Truth the jewel, wrought in rhyme,
Sparkles on the brow of Time;
Gods upon them peace bestow,
Byron, Shelley, Keats, and Poe.

XLIII

Heart, we were so happy then,
    Thou and I, thou and I;
Heart, he seemed the man of men,
And the mountain and the glen
Blossomed into sunshine when,
    Joyous, he came nigh.

Heart, we are so lonely now,
    Thou and I, thou and I;
Gloom is on the mountain's brow,
And, poor heart, we weep enow,
Yet we proudly cherish how
    Did our warrior die.

XLIV
WINTER SONG

The hills where I was wont to go
Are buried in a shroud of snow;
The Ice king holds in fast embrace
The river with her shining face;
The trees, impatient, stand and wait
Summer to ope her golden gate,
But though wild winter doth enfold,---
Our merry hearts are never cold.

The hills again in green will rise
And lift their banners to the skies;
The river burst her frozen thong,
And leap and laugh in joyous song;
Each tree will don his leafy coat,
The robin sing with lusty throat;
Blessings will be most manifold,---
Our merry hearts are never cold!

XLV
AT THE URN

Ida sitteth at the urn,
    Every afternoon at three;
Since that summer at Lucerne
    I am very fond of,---tea;
"Sugar?" "Thank you, just a lump."
    Ah, Pilatus, proud and free,
How my foolish heart goes thump,
    I am very fond of,---tea.

Ida sitteth at the urn,
    "One more cup?" "Why certainly,"
While we watched Swiss sunsets burn,
    I grew very fond of,---tea;
Now we're married, in a flat,
    She paints things, I write you see,
Cheese and kisses, and all that,
    And we're very fond of,---tea.

XLVI
DOVES

At evening in the peaceful grove,
    And in the forest dim,
Where every nook is light with love,
    And every sound a hymn,
The gentle doves, the tender doves,
    Come flying home to rest
Each happy little head upon
    Another happy breast.

At evening on the city pave,
    And in the city street,
With footsteps leading to the grave,
    And to the winding-sheet,
The poor lost doves, the storm toss'd doves,
    The fallen sisters come,
Whose lives are lame, whose souls are shame,
    Alas, who have no home!

XLVII

OFF SANTIAGO
(June, 1898.)

I.

Hobson went towards death and hell,
　　Hobson and his men,
Unregarding shot and shell,
And the rain of fire that fell,
Calm, undaunted, fearless, bold,
Every heart, a heart of gold,
Steadfast, daring, uncontrolled---
　　Hobson and his men.

II.

Hobson came from death and hell,
　　Hobson and his men,
Shout the tidings, ring the bell,
Let the pealing anthems swell,
Back from wreck, and raft, and wave,
From the shadow of the grave,
Every honor to the brave---
　　Hobson and his men.

XLVIII

I bowed to a tree, and his thought unto me
    Was, "Bless you, O bless you, O bless you!"
I smiled at the sky, and the blue seemed to cry,
    "O bless you, O bless you, O bless you!"
I chirped to a bird, and the answer I heard
    Was, "Bless you, O bless you, O bless you!"
I sang everywhere, and the echoing air
    Rang, "Bless you, O bless you, God bless you!"

The mountain and vale, the dell and the dale,
    Proclaim to mankind, "O God bless you!"
The land and the sea, in beauty and glee,
    Forever seem saying, "God bless you!"
The noon and the night, in dreamful delight
    Of sunshine and stars, say, "God bless you!"
A pæon of mirth doth engirdle the earth
    Of "Bless you, O bless you, God bless you!"

XLIX
ODE TO LIBERTY

I.

White as the light of noonday sun,
The name and fame of Washington,
His deeds are writ with loving art
On every page in every heart,
His might men more staunch than oak,
In thunder tones to British spoke,
And from the mountains to the sea
The echoes rang with Liberty.

II.

But never were we wholly free,
Or tasted sweetest liberty,
While from the east to western wave
One mortal called another,--- "Slave!"
But when the civil conflict came,
When from the passion and the flame
The nation rose triumphant, free,
Then knew we sweetest Liberty.

III.

When Lincoln bade a race arise
And look to God with new-born eyes,
This was the day and this the deed,
And Freedom stood unbonneted;
This was the deed and this the day
When all the Blue and all the Gray
Might reunite and sing in glee
Of Liberty, sweet Liberty.

IV.

And now the sun of freedom shines,
And every vine of freedom twines,---
Holding the Union in a grasp,
No earthly power shall unclasp;
No North, no South, no East or West,
But one Republic brave and blest,
Whose song and watchword aye shall be,
Of Liberty, sweet Liberty.

L

All the people of the earth
Have a common death and birth;
All the men beneath the sky
Hope and love as thou and I;
Some are weak and some are strong,
Some are right and some are wrong,
But as dusk is after day,
We must journey in one way.
Of the hosts of humankind,
Some have vision, some are blind,
But the poorest child of fate
Doth outline the kingly state;
Over land and over sea,
Life, and death, and mystery;
Childhood, age, and from the steep,
All must make the final leap,
All must crumble into clay,
In one calm and peaceful way;
To perfect the sacred plan,
Let us love our fellow-man.

LI
TO THE NATIONS

Shame on your craven, crew,
You coward Nations, you!
Sitting supinely by,
While men file out to die;
Glory, you call it,---Shame
Shall be its filthy name!
Lust, pillage, blood, and hate
Envenom all the State;
You call it war,---you do---
Shame on you, Nations---you!

Shame on your sickly crew,
You coward Nations, you!
Prating of God and Peace;---
Go, bid the carnage cease;---
Drag Emperor and Tsar
Before your mighty bar;
Let Love and Mercy reign
Over the land and main;---
You call it war, you do---
Shame on you, Nations---you!

Book II

Being More Echoes

from

The Gates of Silence

with

Interludes of Song

To the memory
of

SAM AND MARGARET

I sent my Soul through the Invisible.

The Rubáiyát

I

Orb after orb, sphere upon sphere,
   Fire-feasting worlds aflame,
In lines of light upon the night,
   Tracing Jehovah's name.

Star calling unto star,
   Across the deeps above,
With one vast voice, "Rejoice, rejoice,
   Jehovah's name is Love."

II

The lily whispered: "From the sod
   I leap into the light;
Thou churlish clod, to doubt thy God,
   Nor know the noon from night.

"Look where I lay, but yesterday,
   O thou of feeble faith,---
So thou shalt climb, and soar sublime
   From the swift pause of death."

III

We stand upon a narrow strip of years,
Time's boundless ocean laying either shore;
One pale expanse behind us, and before
Another sea its vasty bulk uprears;
Out of the submerged centuries doth come,
No hint or whisper of the veilèd plan,
Still o'er the desert winds the caravan
To read the riddle, but the sphinx is dumb.
Man's soul, a restless captive clad in clay,
Sees not beyond the walls of Night and Day;
The wrecks of creeds and dogmas strew the past,
And prophecy is but an idle breath,
To know, we must adventure at the last,
'Neath the grim guidance of the pilot, Death.

IV

What! I fear Death?
  Believe me, no;
Out of a mystery we come,
  Into the light we go.

What! I fear Death?
  I swear to thee,
My chiefest thought is one
  Of curiosity.

V

Deeply dark God's secret dwells,
  Vainly Saint and Psalmist sing;---
All the heavens, all the hells,
  Are of Man's imagining.

Man, who walks in unknown ways,
  Blind beneath the singing skies;
Man, who sucks the dug-drawn days
  Dry of Demons, Deities.

VI

Come, O night, with peace and rest,
    I am ill of day;
Come, O night, upon thy breast,
    Let me drift away;
All the little stars will creep
    Softly lest they mar my sleep,
Every wand'ring wind will weep,
    Come, O gentle Night!

Come, O Death, with rest and peace,
    I am ill of life;
Come, O death, and let us cease
    Love, and joy, and strife;
O'er my grave the breath of June,
    Poppy and the rose aswoon
All the yellow afternoon,
    Come, O gentle Death!

VII

Man, the atom, boldly goes
To battle with his dearest foes;
Man, the atom, doth persuade,
God, is in our image made.

Man, the atom, soars and sings,
Lord of lords, and king of kings;
Then, baffled by dumb, doubting skies;
Man, the atom, bravely dies.

VIII

Fate flings her gauntlet at my feet,
   I boldly lift the gage;
Fear shall not be my company
   Upon the pilgrimage.

Death cannot daunt, nor woe, nor want,
   Nor all the shafts of scorn;
O'er Life's glad day I speed away,
   Mad with its mirth of morn.

IX

Time doth not fly, nor creep, nor crawl, nor run;
"Tis we that move; Time standeth vast and still,
And keepeth ward o'er valley and o'er hill,
While we, like dewdrops in the morning sun,
Gleam and are gone; Oh, say not then that Time
Moves slowly, swiftly; Time is young as when
The first-born of the haughty race of men
Rose up and dared death with a soul sublime.
The Summer, Autumn, Winter, and the Spring
Stand in amaze as we speed wildly by,
And Nature's self is ever-wondering
That we so soon upon her bosom die.
Say not Time goes, 'tis hasting man who flees,
While stand agape the startled centuries.

X

If we must come to naught,
   Yet is it best to be,
There is but one vast thought,---
   "Tis Immortality.

The wild dreams of the soul
   Can never be in vain,
Unto some lofty goal
   Wendeth the mortal train.

XI

O goodly plot of sky and earth,
   Of mountain and of lea,
Of children, roses, sorrow, mirth,
   And bliss and agony.

Ours are the tides of years that flow
   Unto the unknown sea,
Through childhood, frosty age; then ho,
   We set sail for the mystery!

XII

I thought that I had died and, fleet of soul,
Was speeding outward through the realms of Night,
On and yet on I winged my eager flight,
Straining to catch a first glimpse of the goal;
I felt the billows of the darkness roll,
Waving about me in their turgid might;
I prayed to God that but one ray of light
Would glimmer faintly from a friendly knoll;
The clumsy ages slowly crept along,
And still I drifted o'er the unknown way,
Until, afar, I heard seraphic song,
And came where weary pilgrims rest and pray;
Then, then, our child that died at infancy
Came toddling out to kiss and welcome me.

XIII

Two legions battling in the blood
    Are struggling for the soul;
The one of evil, one of good,
    Both grappling for the goal.

One pleading peace, one urging strife,
    Lashed 'twixt the twain am I;
God grant the better angels life,
    Bid the damn'd demons die.

XIV

Poor, hoping, praying, helpless man,
Without a chart, without a plan,
Bound for a voyage on a sea
Of death, of life, of mystery.

Believing all things, knowing naught,
Kings of the mighty realm of thought,
Off for a voyage on a sea
Of dark, of light, of mystery.

XV

The shades of evening softly fall,
Farewell, a long farewell,
Parting must come to one and all,
Farewell, again farewell;
Love like a beacon shines afar,
And Faith is steadfast as a star,
Before us lies the harbor-bar,
Farewell, and then farewell.

Let old Grief hide her aching eyes,
Farewell, dear heart, farewell,
Morning again will light the skies,
Farewell, and then farewell;
Our barque is on the ocean years,
O ebb of joy, O flow of tears,
And gently pealing in our ears,
Farewell, a last farewell!

XVI

This life we know, of bliss and woe,
    Then what will soft unfold;
Ah, sweet the years of loves and fears,
    And youth's mad minted gold.

This life we know but lordly powers,
    Above, below, that be,
What of the voyage that is ours
    Over the unknown sea!

XVII

I do not know, I do not fear,
I only stand amazèdly,
And, down the dawn or nightly sky,
Watch pageants wonderful pass by.

I do not fear, my soul doth hear,
My wild enraptured soul doth see,
'Tis but the curtain rising
On an act that is to be.

XVIII

A thousand years doth Nature plan
Upon the making of a Man;
She sweeps the generations through,
To find the patient, strong, and true;
She rends the surge of seven seas,
Rearing a humble Socrates;
She burns a hundred years of sun,
Sealing the soul of Solomon.

A thousand years doth Nature plan
Upon the making of a Man;
She sees the ages dawn apace,
Ere Moses rouse his shackled race,
Or Homer or sweet Shakespeare sing,
Beside his deep eternal spring;
The centuries rise in reverence when
Buddha doth come unto his men.

A thousand years doth Nature plan
Upon the making of a Man;
She fills his heart with fire and faith,
She leaves him loyal unto death;
She lights his lustrous, loving eye
With flash of immortality;
She adds one more undying name
Upon the heated scroll of Fame.

XIX

Our passion, longing, love, and hate
    Mean something more, mean something more;
Not idly do the winds of fate
    Around us crack and roar.

Our joy and sorrow, bliss and pain,
    Mean something more, mean something more;
Mercy will kiss away the stain
    If that our souls are sullied o'er.

XX

I know when in the last ditch,
    For then I gaily sing,
When poorest, I am rich,
    Burgeons of blossoming.

I know when I am poor,
    And low, and meek, and sad,
God standeth at my door,
    Yearning to make me glad.

XXI

They stand to me, these men of mine,
    Brigaded end to end,
And though we send nor hint nor sign,
    All comprehend.

We raise the crimson falling flanks,
    Ensanguin'd battles done;
Then, in well-knit, beseeming ranks,
    We march from sun to sun.

XXII

God flings the golden days like coins
    Out of his spendthrift hands;
They lie up-piled by centuries
    O'er all the lavish lands.

Old miser Time hoards them away,
    Cunning and carefully;
Perhaps he hopes at last to own
    All of Eternity.

XXIII

One only thing, I hope, I trust,
I know if all my thought is just,
I know if all my deeds are kind,
No future fear can haunt my mind.

I hope, I trust, I feel, I know,
Where'er my soul may groping go,
Or through the shadow, or the night,
At last, it must, it will be light.

XXIV

I hunted heaven everywhere,
    I blindly sought for solace sweet,
While shyly peeping unaware,
    Meek daisies nestled at my feet.

I cried aloud for hint of God,
    Telling my beaded baubles o'er,
While from the quick womb of the sod,
    Glad roses climbed to deck my door.

XXV

At the end of the land of joy and pain,
    We come to the little gate;
The king and the clown, and the court go down
    Through its portals soon or late;
The peasant, the peer, the sage, and the seer
    Depart when the day comes round,
With a muffled cry and a last good-by,
    Out through the gate in the ground.

Tis fix'd by fate, we must pass the city gate,
    Little clay gate in the ground,
At the end of our ways of nights and days,
    'Tis marked by a grassy mound;
We bend o'er the bier with a sob and tear,
    And the still lips give no sound;
We never can know where God's gardens grow,
    But through the gate in the ground.

THE END.

The Blushful South and Hippocrene:

Being Songs

Originally published in 1909

O for a beaker full of the warm South,
Full of the true, the blushful Hippocrene,
With beaded bubbles winking at the brim
    And purple-stainèd mouth;

                Keats

CONTENTS
THE BLUSHFUL SOUTH AND HIPPOCRENE

THE DREAMS

Only the dreams are real,
    The false facts fade and die;
The rare rose-lipp'd ideal
    Defies eternity.

Only the dreams are real,
    Only the dreams endure;
Let thy soul's white ideal
    Be ever true and pure.

SONG

Odors of oceans sleep deep in her hair,
Skies of young summers dream warm in her eyes,
      Lo, I must go to her,
      Tell my vast woe to her,
Hold her, and fold her, and crush her with love;
      Night is where she is not,
      Pain, sorrow, stain, and blot---
Love, O my Love, come thou in unto me;
Learn'd in love's lore, thou art wise, thou art wise,
Kiss'd by love's lips, thou art fair, thou art fair,
      Let me no longer pine,
      Love, O Love, be thou mine,
Heart of my heart, haste thou now unto me.

EVENING SONG

Night is as a deep black rose,
    Steep'd in sweets to the lees,
Full of the loves and woes
    Of swarming starry bees.

Lo, now, upon the air,
    Forth from her dusk cocoon,
Fragile, and faint, and fair,
    Flutters the white moth moon.

YESTERDAY RAN ROSES

Yesterday ran roses,
    To-day it is the rue;
Again, again, O Love, I swear
    To be strong and true.

To-day it is the cowl and fast,
    To-morrow, what will be?
Foolish heart, hast not enough
    Of pain and ecstasy?

TO HIS BOOK

Go little book to every heart,
Woo them, win them with thine art.

Go little book to every eye,
Begging crumbs of sympathy.

Stay little book against each breast,
That promises to give thee rest.

Come little book again to me,
If no soft bosom welcome thee.

My fond heart shall hold a nook,
Ever for thee, little book.

IN THE PALE WOODS

In the pale woods at early dawn,
   The tearful trees dripp'd dew,
The soft, shy shadows, waking wan,
   Murmured of you, of you.

I climbed to sunlit heights at eve,
   Triumphant, steadfast, and true;
Festooning crimson, banner'd blue.---
   Thinking of you, of you.

THE DAYS

The glad days fly so merrily,
The glad days dance so cheerily,
O for to fling a loop of gold,
And every hoyden moment hold!

The sad days droop so drearily,
So wan-eyed and so wearily,
O for a cat-o'-nine-tails then
To lash the laggards on again!

ROSE SONG

I.

Yellow rose go to her,
Breathe all my woe to her,
Mellow rose, tell her my hope and despair;
Swear my wild vow to her
To the calm brow of her,
Drawn in tempestuous deeps of her hair.

II.

Crush'd in the arms of her,
Thou shalt know balms of myrrh,
Rose, O, rare rose, to my Lady, away!
Waft, where I wait for her,
Love, and love's fate for her,
Haste thee, rose, haste, to my Lady, I pray!

IN GOD'S ACRE

The beggar and the king
   Sleep softly side by side,
Death unto each doth bring
   A grave thus deep, thus wide.

The peasant and the peer
   Are of a kindred clay,
Resting in silence here,
   After life's little day.

SONG

What cannot the poet do?
Hiving wisdom's honey-dew?
What cannot the poet see,
By white truth's immensity?

With the fulcrum of a song,
He can spin the world along,
With a lyric for a lever,
He may stride the stars forever.

SONG

    Sing it away,
    Fling it away,
    Laugh it away,
    Quaff it away;
Let not blear-eyed Sorrow sit
At thy hearth-stone: Throttle it!

    Drive it away,
    Shrive it away,
    Shout it away,
    Rout it away;
Come thou virgin Joy and be
Life, and love, and light to me.

I SHALL MAKE A BRAVE DEATH

I shall make a brave death,
    Spite of hell and all;
I shall with my parting breath,
    Hold pale fate in thrall.

I shall make a brave death,
    Stand thou by and see
How old comrade Life and I
    Can part company.

LOVE

We lack love; if we have love
    We have all in all,
Earth below and stars above,
    And calm and carnival.

Love makes the ringed world ours,
    We are peers of God,
Love woos and makes the flowers,
    Dew-drowsing 'neath the sod.

SONG

Come and let us sing,
    We are growing young,
All the snows of spring,
    Melt upon the tongue;
All the tender lays,
    Laura,---Petrarch's woe,
In the summer days
    Of long ago.

Come and let us sing,
    You and I again.
Let the swift days bring
    Joy, or peace, or pain;
Come and let us sing,
    Love, or bliss, or tears,
Life is on the wing,
    Speeding up the years.

TO-DAY

Though the murk past be blotted out,
    And the pale future robed in mist,
To-day smiles o'er the rabbled rout,
    A virgin yet by time, unkissed.

To-day, to-day, I have to-day---
    Let spectral yesterdays abide,
And ghostly morrows fade away,
    To-day sits blushing by my side.

TO CERBERUS

Thou triple-headed hound beside
    The brazen gates of hell!
Come watch before the portals wide
    Of my soul's citadel.

Here burns a sullen, fiercer fire,
    Oceans can ne'er subdue;
Ambition, passion, love desire,
    Molten to one vast hue.

AUTUMN SONG

There's a calm and tender feeling, as of Autumn in the
    air,
        Ev'rywhere, ev'rywhere;
The shallop leaves sail down, crimson'd green and
    golden'd-brown,
        Here and there, here and there;
Old Rocky Face is sad, haughty, handsome, stern and
    bad,
        But the young Cohuttas smile,
        Dreaming softly all the while,
With the calm and tender feeling, as of Autumn in the
    air.

There's a tender, holy feeling, as of Autumn in the air,
        'Tis a prayer, 'tis a prayer;
Sweet benedictions and all blessings beam upon us,
        Ev'rywhere, ev'rywhere;
While memories of Summer now faintly fade away,
        Hill and valley sing in glee,
        "O, let Love the harvest be,"
With the tender, holy feeling, as of Autumn in the air.

THE MYSTERY

We know a bird, we know a tree,
   We comprehend the sky,
The violet smiles up as we
   Go softly singing by.

We map the land, and chart the sea,
   Feel Nature's pulse and plan,
The one bewild'ring mystery,
   Is myriad-minded man.

A PRAYER

What for the fagot's flame?
   What for the hate and wrong?
Lord God, I bless Thy name,
   I, suffering, am strong.

But, Father in Thy grace,
   Keep from woe's wild unrest,
The woman and the baby face,
   Soft pillowed on her breast.

SONG

Why shouldn't a song
   Be cheery and bright,
If you love it along
   All the day and the night?
If you cuddle it close
   Ere it taketh its flight
And joyously goes
   On the wings of delight.

Why shouldn't a life
   Be free as a song,
Unembittered by strife
   And unclouded by wrong?
O my heart be thou pure,
   O my soul be thou strong---
As the hills that endure,
   As the mountains that throng!

DREAM-PHANTOMS

In the bright light of night,
    Illuming the gloom,
Dream-phantoms weave their flight
    Up from the tomb.

In the deep dark of day,
    Dun-blanketing the light,
Dream-phantoms wing away
    Back to the night.

THE DYING PEARL

Banished from her warm breast,
    Where I was wont to lie,
Torn from my love-blown nest,
    O wretched pearl am I!

Because he proved untrue,
    My mistress cast me by,
Alas, what can I do,
    But lustre-pining die?

THE WOMAN

God send the woman by my way,
She shall possess me night and day,
In her dear eyes my own shall see
All heaven in epitome.

God send the woman by my way,
To her my soul will kneel and pray,
She may allay with her sweet art
The hell that rages in my heart.

WORM DUST

Fat with the fertile dust of man,
   Earth waxeth rich and strong,
To feed her full, since time began,
   The teeming millions throng.

Into her mighty maw we go,
   A gasp, a groan, a squirm;---
Doth old relentless Nature know
   Man from another worm?

SONG

Heliotrope and mignonette,
    Violet and rose,
Madrigal and canzonet,
    Every bloom that blows;
All the happy birds there be,
    Singing through the air,
Whisper, O my Love, of thee,
    Sweet and fond and fair.

Every star upon the sky,
    Bubbling, beaming bright,
Kindles at thy sparkling eye,
    'Tis there fount of light;
Every beauty-breathing gem,
    On the land or sea,
I'd crush into a diadem
    Fit for crowning thee.

SONG

Musical, mystical, low
   A song in the air everywhere,
A wave that doth flow to and fro,
   A note that doth float here and there;
About us, above, and beyond,
   Some melody lureth away,
A symphony tender and fond,
   A rhapsody, jocund and gay.

Yearning, and burning, and sweet,
   A song in the air everywhere,
An aria fervent and fleet,
   A miserere lonely and bare;
Behind us, before, and between,
   We see, and we feel, and we hear,
A rainbow-robed, glorious pæon,
   Enravishing heart, soul, and ear.

THE YOUTH-IMMORTAL

We must wax old and bent,
   Mumble and feebly creep,
We must lie prone and spent,
   Cast on the shore of sleep.

And while our bodies fade,
   To dusty, dim decay,
The earth sweeps rose-array'd,
   On youth-immortal way.

SUN SONG

Drunken with wine of sun,
   I tipple, reel, I sway,
The lewd dark being done,
   I drain another day.

Lapp'd to the lips in light,
   Mad as the roaring seas,
Live long, thou tubbèd wight,
   O rare Diogenes!

SONG

The dream is o'er, and we awake;
    The morn is sweet and fair,
Deep in the purple-scented brake,
    A bird song woos the air;
Up the glad causeway of the east
    The sun leaps evermore,
Anon the noon shall spread her feast---
    Dear Love, the dream is o'er.

The dream is o'er, we did not deem,
    Dear Love, the stars would fade,
We did not deem 'twas but a dream
    Of youth all undismayed.
Look, where adown the saffron west
    Day leads her royal train;
Within mine arms, upon my breast,
    Come, Love, and dream again.

DAWN AND DUSK

I.

A star swoons in the purple east,
    The moon wanes in the west forlorn,
The birds and bees wake for the feast
    Of sunshine, and of mellow morn.

II.

Now o'er uncharted deeps of dark,
    The fire-fly speeds his fragile bark,
Piloted by the self-same One,
    Who guides the chariot of the sun.

THE DAYS

Evasive, evanescent, shy,
    The days of diamond go by,
A string of jewels white they lie
    Between nude nights of ebony.

Unbroken, vast, the chain doth spread
    About the living, and the dead,
Time stands upon the morrow's brink,
    Weaving another lucent link.

SONG

Let the lute, and the flute, and viol leap
    In trancèd ecstasies;
And the train of a royal music sweep
    Before our avid eyes;
Let the old songs come from the tender past,
    Yearning with passion's pain,
Sweet trumpeter sound forth a martial blast,
    Calling to arms again.

Let a pageant pass o'er the fragrant grass,
    Of virgins lithe and free,
And each wistful maid, be she all arrayed
    In folds of melody;
Let the chorus wake for the old sake's sake,
    Our hearts forego their care,
Till the day and the night, in wild delight,
    Echo the rapture rare.

SONG

Dear day, fond day,
Haste thee not away,
All the world is fragrant,
With incense of the May;
All the hills are happy,
Every dale is gay,
As in a dream, the mountain stream,
Ripples its roundelay.

Sweet day, good day,
Linger yet I pray,
Every beatific bush,
The wind doth gently sway;
In my heart I'll bear thee,
All my life along;
In commemoration,
Seal thee in a song.

OBLIVION

I cast my soul against the wall,
I saw it writhe, and cringe, and fall,
I smote it fiercely hip and thigh,
I watched it die in agony.

Now I can face the tides of years,
Freed of those dumb, foreboding fears,
Now while the ages rumble on,
I can know deep oblivion.

SONG

I.
To me they are primroses,
    For that they're sweet and prim,
Shy hidden in the closes
    Of cloisters cool and dim.

II.
O modest, fond primroses,
    Let me thy lover limn
Thy swayings, nods, and poses,
    Into a primrose hymn.

SONG

'Tis in the rose, 'tis in the thorn,
'Tis in the midnight, and the morn;
It dimples in a drop of dew,
Or beameth in the ocean's blue;
'Tis here, 'tis there, 'tis everywhere,
From Zuider Zee to Zanzibar;
No race or region, coast or clime,
That sees not Beauty's self sublime.

'Tis in the rushlight, and the star,
'Tis there, 'tis here, 'tis near and far,
It came with chaos, and will go
With our proud planet's overthrow;
Poor, poor is he, who cannot see
Earth's sweetness and simplicity;
Beauty, the lavish, royal king,
Hath set his seal on everything.

SONG

I.

When fortune flung me flowers,
  Of fragrance and delight,
Through all the golden hours,
  I held their sweetness slight.

II.

And now if fate doth dole me,
  Once in the rose-reft years,
A shy bloom to console me,
  I nourish it with tears.

THE HOLLOW YEARS

Our follies and our weaknesses
  Creep from the past to vex our eyes,
They taunt us, haunt us, flaunt us,
  With their mocking memories.

Out of the hollow years they come,
  Old serpent ghosts of wrongs we wrought,
Writhing in pain within the brain,
  Coiling themselves about our thought.

SONG

Sing to the sorrow, Dear,
    Lift thy sweet eyes of light,
Luminous, loving, clear,
    Deep as the pools of night;
Come let us wear the woe,
    Tenderly, trustfully, now,
Grief, like a dream shall go,
    Peace, sit enthron'd on thy brow.

Wear now the sorrow, Dear,
    Calm like a dawn shall kiss,
The threat'ning clouds of fear,
    Banish'd by winds of bliss;
Come let us fold the woe,
    Like some fond garment away,
Love, O dear Love, come go,
    Bravely to welcome the day.

THE HIDDEN GOAL

I.

I said unto my soul,
   "If thou art more than clay,
Point me the hidden goal,
   Light me the trackless way."

II.

Send but one shred of light,
   One wisp whereon to cling,
E'er sealed in sodden night,
   I lie a clodden thing.

SONG

The glad earth sings it to the sky,
   The stars unto the sea;
A violet with a moistened eye
   Can whisper it to me.

Old night doth know, young day could tell,
   O doubting, fearing man,
King Love doth reign, that all is well,
   That we shall live again.

SONG

Peace hover at my heart,
    Sweet peace, come clasp me now,
Play thy quiescent part,
    And soothe my burning brow;
Come take me to thy breast,
    Smooth all my cares away,
Fold me in robes of rest,
    Guide me the stilly way.

Lo I have wandered long,
    Across the sunlit wold,
Singing my bravest song,
    Youth sped, and I am old;
O tender spirit, Peace,
    Come nestle at my soul;
Bid sorrow now surcease,
    Mellow the evening goal.

THE SEARCH

I want to see, when he doth die,
How careless, brave, and free,
He'll step into the mystery,---
He swore he'd look for me.

And I shall wing from place to place,
And climb the last redoubt;
We twain will rend the womb of space,
Seeking each other out.

I ONLY KNOW

Impartial, calm, submissive, I
Watch silently beneath the sky;
Sworn to swift doubts that ebb and flow,
I only know, I do not know.

Fantastic, puerile, and vain,
Chaff winnow'd from man's dusty brain
Is all surmise; We come, we go,---
I only know, I do not know.

LIKE A LITTLE CHILD

If one had a heart like a little child,
Tender, and innocent, and mild,
And could see the world through a joyous mind,
Gentle, and pure, and sweet, and kind,
There were then no sorrow and passion wild,
If one had a heart like a little child.

Poetry, Love, and Truth would reign,
And the years be free of regret and pain,
Laughter and mirth, and peace and light,
And the sunshine day, and the tranquil night;
Better than fame and wealth up-piled,
Is to have a heart like a little child.

A BALLADE OF LIVING LADIES

Mary and Maud and Kate,
    Jennie and Julia and Bess,
These it has been my fate,
    To love, and to kiss, and caress;
Dora and Flora and May,
    Lettie and Hetty and Eve,
How so? well, I never can say,
    But I worship'd them all, I believe.

Phyllis and Fanny and Grace,
    Sybil and Sallie and Sue,
God bless each sunshiny face,
    Ah, I was ardent to woo;
Ellen and Helen and Rose,
    Enid and Edna and Pearl,
Damn me, you will, I suppose,
    But I burn'd and yearn'd for each girl.

ENVOI

Prince, how in the devil is it,
    Through all of love's fever and fret,
As often as I have been smit,
    Lo, I am a bachelor yet?

THE HOLLOW CROWN

If I could drive this demon down,
    And tent him to the quick,
Could I renounce the hollow crown,
    That makes me heretic;

If my bared brow might face the sun,
    Again, again, I vow;---
What! I chose thee, thou Lucifer,
    Leering upon me now?

THE VAST PORTENT

If we thought what honor meant,
    Wisdom, faith and truth,
If we dreamed the vast portent
    Bulb'd in age and youth;

If we touch'd a syllable
    Or of death, or life,
Heaven would spring from ev'ry hell,
    Love from every strife.

SONG

The poet waits beside the gates,
    Of Dreamland's paradise,
No other goal can lure his soul,
    No other scene his eyes.
Nor weal nor woe, nor ebb nor flow,
    Can tempt him to arise;
But still he waits beside the gates,
    Of Dreamland's paradise.

Within is light, without is night,
    And emptiness and void,
Within is life, without is strife,
    And sorrow unalloyed.
And through the years of hopes and fears,
    And prayers and agonies,
The poet waits beside the gates,
    Of Dreamland's paradise.

O poet-soul, while ages roll,
    Upon the shores of time,
No other bliss is like a kiss,
    From holy lips of rhyme,
No joy so rare in earth or air,
    Or in star-shotten skies,---
The poet waits beside the gates,
    Of Dreamland's paradise.

SONG

My song's for thee,
    Dear Love, I pray,
Dost thou not see
    In all I say?
The soul of me?
    O Love, I bring
Myself to thee
    In all I sing.

For thee, for thee,
    Each thought, each word;
Love's melody
    If still unheard,
Soon dies in sighs;
    O Love, to thee,
I bring, I sing,
    Love's ecstasy.

THE TRAIL OF LIFE

The trail of life leads out and far away,
We follow blindly for a little day;
And then our baffled brethren take it up,
Till they, too, drain the dark draught of death's cup.

The trail of life leads out and far away,
A sip of sorrow and a gleam of gay,
A feast of love, some bitter brew of wrath,
All follow blindly in the beaten path.

LOVE

I have not love, or I should see
A heart and soul in every tree;
I have not love, or any rose
Would breathe its fragrant woes to me;
I have not love, or I could hear
The might music of the sphere;
I have not love, or God would be
A God, and not a mystery.

I have not love, or I should go
Singing unto the gates of woe;
I have not love, or death would seem
A joy, a rapture, and a dream;
I have not love, or man would be
Sworn friend and brother unto me;
I have not love, or I should see
That Life is love and sympathy.

I have not love, or hell and night
Would vanish into living light;
I have not love, or grief and gloom
Would flower into happy bloom;
I have not love, I have not love---
But the poor falling crumbs thereof;
Fortune doth fade, and pleasures pall,
But Love is all, and all, and all.

SOME POWER DIVINE

Some power divine hath rear'd its shrine
   Within my soul, O mighty man,
Its altars rise to greet the skies,
   O'er all the years its arches span.

Some purpose vast pursues the past,
   Some high fate meets the dawning day,
The gorgeous scheme, a pulsing dream,
   With hope, lights life's triumphant way.

O brother, clasp in loving grasp
   The hand thy kinsman holds to thee,
With truth for guide, come boldly ride
   Abreast to God, and victory.

SONG

The words are mute,
So let the lute,
O let the music tell
The dreams that dwell
    Within my soul,
And touch my heart to tears;
     O Love, who art my goal,
Heed thou my hopes and fears.

The words are vain,
So let some strain
Within the music plead,
E'en while doth bleed
    The singer's soul;
O Love, my heart for thee,
    Clad all in samite stole,
Is dumb with ecstasy.

SONG

I.

The music waits the words,
  On portals rare of bliss,
The music waits the words,
  See how they clasp and kiss.

II.

The words go nobly forth,
  To touch her garment's hem,
Lo, now they meet, and look,
  Joy doth encompass them.

III.

O happy thought and strain,
  Immortal, royal, free,
Through longing, passion, pain,
  Mated in melody.

SONG

Of all the dear dreams that possess me,
    Of all the fond fancies that come,
The sweetest are those that caress me,
    With visions and pictures of home;
Afar from my hearth-side I wander,
    O'er oceans of billow and foam,
And peace seems to me only yonder,
    Beneath my own roof-tree of home.

A truce to the tinsel of travel,
    Farewell to the palace of kings,
No longer I care to unravel
    Strange threads from the garment of things;
I shall go to my own like the swallow,
    Saint Peter's may cherish its dome,
My heart's in the South and I follow,
    The South, and my hearth-side of home.

SONG FOR ALL SOULS

God bless all poor souls to-day,
Those who weep or those who pray;
Those who sing or those who sigh
Underneath the roof-tree sky;
North, or east, or far, or near,
Kinsmen linkèd by a tear.

Thou, that art my brother, say
God bless all poor souls to-day.

God bless all poor souls to-day,
Love alone doth reign always;
Bold or brave, or weak, or worn,
Jewel-decked or tatter-torn;
Beggar, prince, or clown or king,
Weeping bird with bruisèd wing.

All within Love's sov'ran sway,---
God bless all poor soul's to-day.

MOUNTAIN SONG

I cried unto the mountain,
    "What art thou
    With thy brow
Soothed, and smoothed, and kissed, and caressed
At the fountain of the sky, of the sky?"

"Are the clouds that cling about thee,
Are the winds that sing about thee,
    Robe and voice;
    Dost rejoice,
In thy station of elation upon high?"

The mountain spake to me,
    "O thou child,
    Wayward, wild,
Be thou strong in storm and calm,
Peace will pour its oil of balm
    O'er the waters of thy soul;
    And the goal, O the goal,
Of glory there up-piled,
    Thou shalt grasp it,
    Thou shalt clasp it,
O my child, O my child."

SONG

O youth, happy youth,
   How I long to seize thee,
Frolic youth, in goodly truth,
   Tell why I displease thee;
Thou art mirthful, wild, and fair,
Dews of morn besprink thy hair;
And thy fragrant beauty pure,
Ever, ever, doth endure;
O youth, tender youth,
   Pray thee, do not leave me,
Bide anear, the song to hear,
   That my soul doth weave thee.

O youth, trusting youth,
   Ardent youth believe me,
If thy heart doth harbor truth,
   Love can never leave thee;
Each last longing in thy breast,
Still shall be the loveliest;
Each dream-flower of thy mind,
Sway unto a sweeter wind;
Youth, youth, immortal youth,
   Stay thee, pray thee, hear me,
Go not now, alas I vow,---
   Ever bide anear me.

BEAUTY SEEMED AFAR

Beauty seemed afar,
    As the faintest star,
Beauty looked to be,
    All-where, but with me.

I love Beauty so
    That I sought her face
Where I chanced to go,
    Dank, or dreary place;

And I found her there,
    In the dunnest night
I could stroke her hair,
    I could feel the light.

Now close at my side,
    Beauty evermore
Like a joyous bride
    Tells my blisses o'er.

Hand in hand we fare,
    Up the rhyme-lit years
Half the day in rapture rare,
    Half the night in tears.

SONG

I fancy I hear Nancy,
   Slipping softly down the stair,
Creeping slyly up behind me,
   Just to catch me unaware,
And I close my eyes, and seem to doze
   Within my great arm-chair,
So that Nancy, whom I fancy,
   Now may think me sleeping there.

I fancy it is Nancy,
   Who doth stand behind me now,
And doth press her warm lips lightly,
   Twice and thrice upon my brow;
And I wake and take her captive,
   And the ransom that I claim,
Is that Nancy, whom I fancy,
   Must instanter take my name.

SONG

There's never a lass for me,
    Alas, alas for me!
There's never a maid, I am afraid,
To seek my slippers, rub my head,
And light my poor old bones to bed,
    Alas, alas for me!

There's never a lass for me,
    Alas, alas for me!
Such is my plight, I long to fight;
No woman's kiss to make me glad,
No blessèd bairn to call me "Dad,"
    Alas, alas for me!

There's never a lass for me,
    Alas, alas for me!
I care not I, to live or die,---
Why---Mary---dear, I wrote the rhyme
The morn we met; ah happy time
    There is a lass for me.

SONG

I came to the mill, by the little high hill,
The big wheel turned, Love you, I love you;
The river ran down, past they lazy old town,
Singing, Love you, O love you, I love you;
Each tree waved a limb, and the wind hummed a hymn
Of, Love you, O love you, I love you,
And as onward I went, all the breezes unbent,
Blowing, Love you, O love you, I love you.

O rock, bush, and tree, and winds brave and free,
I love you, O love you, I love you;
Joy, sorrow, sweet tears, and swift speeding years,
I love you, O love you, I love you;
O life, and O death, O beauty, and breath,
I love you, O love you, I love you;
By land and by sea, a voice unto me,
Sings, Love you, O love you, I love you.

THE LABOR OF THE CHILD

I.

Shut the from the light of day,
 Dividends, dividends;
Rob them of their youth and play,
 Dividends, dividends;
Stunt and dwarf the coming race,
Flabby limb and bloodless face,---
A prison mill, an infant's place---
 Dividends! Dividends!

II.

Steal their freedom and their joy,
 Dividends, dividends;
Sacrifice the girl and boy,
 Dividends, dividends;
Foolish, blind, impotent State,
Sowing dragon teeth of hate---
Save thy nurslings from this fate---
 Dividends! Dividends!

ROSE SONG

The Rose will give a party
  To the Butterfly and Bee,
Everybody will eat hearty,
  For the honey is all free;
  Free, free, free,
  Everything is free,
Flower flagons filled with honey,
  For the Butterfly and Bee.

The Humming-bird will be there,
  And all the Dragon-flies,
O the fun they all will see there,
  Underneath the Summer skies.
  Summer, Summer skies,
  Underneath the Summer skies;
O the fun they all will see there,
  Humming-birds and Dragon-flies.

THE QUEST

He died, and through the yearning years,
    He swept illimit space,
Searching 'mid roll of reeling spheres,
    Peering in ev'ry face.

Seeking with heart and soul aflame,
    And spirit steeped in woe,
The woman he had sent to shame,
    In olden long ago.

At last lock'd in each other's eyes,
    Sweet Mercy bade them go,
On through the star-strewn centuries,
    Made pure by love and woe.

ZOLA

Against thy weakness and thy shame,
Poor, flighty France, the noble name
Of Zola stands, who for the right,
Hath dared thy myrmidons of might.

A patient world impatient waits,
That justice reign within thy gates,
O France, by cruel error led,
In deep dishonor hang thy head!

Woe to the nation or the State,
That cloaks a crime, that harbors hate;
Her pride, her pomp, her people must
Be crushed and humbled to the dust.

France, let this evil be undone!
Hear thou the pleading of thy son,
Thy Zola, who hath writ his name
In love, upon the scroll of fame!

Paris, 1898

SONG

Flora is a famous flirt,
   Well I know,
And she doeth grievous hurt,
   And she worketh woe;
O, her soft and tender sighs,
O, her sweet and gentle eyes,
Where the tearful rivers rise,
   And I love her so!

Flora is a famous flirt,
   Alack-a-day!
I would swear by her hair,
   By her bosom pray;---
Of all the women she is best,
I but call her flirt in jest,
When I clasp her to my breast,
   And I love her so!

TO LOVE

The god of all the gods that be is Love,
He reigneth over bond and free,
His pinions spread o'er land and sea,
O'er mountain and o'er grove;
No monarch but must bend the knee
Unto this nobler king;
No soul so poor, if he hath love,
He lacks not anything;
Day dawns for love, and night doth tell
His glory to the wond'ring stars;
The sun doth rise and set for love,
And dreaming on her evening way,
The moon resumes the silver theme;
A toast to Love, at ev'ry feast,
He should be first and chiefest guest,
And o'er all be supreme;
All you who love and have been loved,
Come, fill your cup to Love!

THE END.

On the Way to Willowdale

Being Other

Songs from a
Georgia Garden

With

Sonnet Interludes

Originally published in 1912

INDEX TO FIRST LINES

SONG

Here in this quiet bower,
   Here in this sweet retreat,
Where the shower of the flower
   Is fragrant at my feet,
Here all the day, I sing away
   The wild hope-haunted hour,
Beneath the old tall tower,
   Here in this happy bower.

Here in this castle airy,
   I weave my jocund dreams,
Young Cupid is the fairy
   Of all the singing streams;
Miss Venus grieves amid the leaves,
   Adonis will not tarry,
My Pan doth plan that maid and man,
   And everybody marry.

SONG

The red rose burns my passion,
    The white rose weeps my woe,
All the flowers in a fashion
    Sympathize and seem to know;
The myrtle dons her kirtle,
    The buttercup her gown,
And bleeding-heart essays a part,
    To set the symptoms down.

The gentian I must mention,
    And silken poppy too,
The crocus, (hokus pokus)
    Says it's silly so to woo;
If they think that they know better,
    I'll keep my counsel still,
Let each blossom be a letter,
    And tell her what they will.

SONG

A Butterfly came gaily
    Into the garden close,
A dozen meet there daily
    To gossip with the Rose;
The Hummingbird was lightly stirred
By every honey word he heard,
And when the Dragon-fly flew by,
The Beetle's baby 'gan to cry.

Oh, my children, O, my children,
    Look out and see the show,
Just listen to them glisten
    As they blithely come and go;
I'll plant a little garden
    Without a sprig of fear,
And all the day will be so gay,
    You'ld play there all the year.

SONG

The Blue-jay is a fellow
   Who is busy all the day,
The Sparrow is quite narrow
   In his views, the others say;
The Cardinal is crimson
   With rapture and delight,
The Thrush maintains a hermit hush,
   The Owl is up at night.

The Pecker-wood is understood
   By every stalking hawk,
The Robin's heart is throbbing,
   You may know it by his walk;
It really is exciting,
   With joy my soul is stirred,
I can't do any writing
   For thinking of a bird.

SONG

The periwinkle softly said,
   "I love the snug old earth,"
The lilac laughed in lavender
   And added fragrant mirth;
My Lady donned a purple gown,
   And came along just then,
The clover, nettle, violet,
   Empurpled all the glen.

The people all wore purple,
   The sky was purple too,
Beneath a purple petticoat
   There peeped a purple shoe;
As it became a cavalier,
   Of tyrian dye my vest;
I wound a chain of purple pearls
   And bound them 'round her breast.

HASCHISH

I cried, "Bring Helen here," and she of Troy,
    In all her glory, came at my command,
    Semiramis I summon'd with a wand,
To stir my pulses with a subtle joy;
And that my rapture might have no alloy,
    Her am'rous eyes by Libyan breezes fann'd,
    The serpent of old Nile from lotus land
Knelt ductile to my touch as any toy;
I ravaged ev'ry century and clime
    To taste the thrill the other mad-men knew
Who hung their hearts before the gaze of Time,
    Deep draining down delirious love's brew;
Now I am too, immortal, while I feel
The poison passion o'er my senses steal.

SONG

Good-morning, Sally Dahlia,
   Said Miss Mary Marigold,
It will be an early autumn
   So the bees to me have told;
The happy Jap chrysanthemums
   Are waving in the wind,
O thank you, Sally Dahlia,
   You are very, very kind.

Good-evening, Mary Marigold,
   Miss Sally Dahlia said,
I'm weepy, creepy, sleepy,
   I should really be in bed;
The Humming-bird is coming
   On the morrow, well I know,
Good-evening, Mary Marigold,
   Sally Dahlia whispered low.

SONG

A Blue-jay and a cat-bird
    Can never quite agree,
I think the row, most often
    Is about the family tree;
Their in-laws get into the muss,
    And raise a merry din,
In-laws are often outlaws,
    When they hang around your bin.

A Humming bird's a bumming bird,
    A slumming bird, a strumming bird,
He goeth like a lightning flash,
A whirl, a zip, a dive, a dash;
The bashful blossoms see him there,
A swift bronze bubble in the air,
And every flower's soul is stirred
With passion for the Humming bird.

SONG

The mocking bird is prince of all
   The happy songster tribe,
His joy is so ecstatic,
   That he should be a scribe,
And set his music unto words,
   So we could something know
Of all his pain and passion,
   Of all his bliss and woe.

He sings by night, he sings by day,
   Eager, alert, and trim,
And every note that floats his way
   He weaves into a hymn;
All the rare random music
   Of the heavy-hanging woods,
He stores within his soul to pour
   On moonlit solitudes.

SONG

Just slip me to a sunbeam,
    Hand me a dram of dew,
I'm drunken with the noonday,
    I need a cooling brew;
Last night I reeled among the stars,
    Dawn came---I swam the east,
What royal dish or dessert,
    Shall be postlude to the feast?

Day darkens to the westward,
    Another eve is nigh,
I'll warm me at the sunset,
    To get my garments dry;
Then in a holy frenzy,
    That must possess me soon,
Away I'll go, muffled and slow,
    To masses at the moon.

SONG

Such another day
    Have I never seen,
All the joyous country way
    Laughs in living green;
Every lusty lark and jay
    Doth his plumage preen,
Heart of mine, the month is May,
    And the lass of is Jean.

May the month, and Jean the lass,
    Oh, the magic moon!
In April, Lucia like a fuchsia,
    Who will come in June?
Will it be dark Carlotta,
    With her kisses manifold,
Or the silken siren Irene,
    With her high heap'd hair of gold?

HIS COMET

Unnamed, a vagrant of the night and stars,
 He drew his train of fire athwart the sky;
 The sons of science passed him coldly by,
The savage saw but pestilence and wars;
Beyond the bounds of Jupiter and Mars,
 He sped where love and duty bade him hie;
 Copernicus' or Galileo's eye
Dared penetrate the mist-obscuring bars;
Then Halley came and plucked his comet down,
 Said, "Go thou now, return on such a day,
Be thou no more a wanderer unknown,
 Assume thy rightful realm in solar sway;"---
Deep dreaming in the dust where Halley lies,
His comet flames his fame along the skies.

SONG

The bride rose sighed all morning,
    The lily loved all day,
The clematis climbed whitely
    Upon her fragrant way;
A butterfly in white came by
    And poised across the air,
High overhead, magnolias spread
    White fragrance everywhere.

It was time for penitence,
    The snowy pigeons came.
Amid the sweet-alyssum
    Murmuring Mary's name:
A child in robe of purity
    Led us in prayer contrite,
We shrived our souls in sunbeams,
    And sang a song of white.

SONG

On thy breast let me rest,
   In thine arms let me lie,
Day dies in the west,
   And the little stars peep;
The eve draweth nigh,
   The soft shadows creep,
To thine arms I would hie,
   On thy breast I would sleep.

Hold me love, fold me love,
   To thy hungering heart,
The wan moon above
   On her voyage doth start;
All the night she doth beam
   In the slumbering sky,---
In thy arms let me dream,
   On thy breast let me lie.

SONG

A fiddle for the merry men,
   A riddle for the wise,
Come fling the happy rose leaves
   Up to the laughing skies;
The theorem ad nauseam,
   Is not for you or me,
We dance on high with butterfly,
   We frolic with the bee.

The peonies are prating,
   Hasten, they will not wait;
The cardinals are mating---
   'Tis an affair of state;
All other facts are minor,
   This is a time for bliss,
Fedora, what is finer
   Than just a hug and kiss?

SONG

The radiant Morning Glory
    Is a glory of the morn,
With honey-suckle neighbors
    Blowing trumpets in the corn.
Some are red, and white, and blue,
Patriotic through and through,
O, the gracious Morning Glories
    Are a glory of the morn.

The mystic pale Moon-flower
    Is a glory of the night,
With fire-flies flitting 'round her
    Like meteors of light;
The moth is nigh, the bat goes by,
    In mad tumultuous flight,
The dreamful white Moon-flowers
    Are a glory of the night.

SONG

Out of the heapèd sorrow
    Pluck the toy of joy,
From grief's mint heaps borrow,
    Gold without alloy;
Dredge with deeps of agony
    Pearls of lucent bliss;
Catch a note of Philomel
    In a serpent's hiss.

From the tree of torture,
    Cull the rose, content;
Ne'er importune fortune
    For good or evil sent;
All are one, and one is all,
    Yestermorns or morrows,---
Pluck the aureate toys of joys,
    From the foolish sorrows.

KEATS

Fair English lad, in thought and dream, a Greek,
    Dead in the blush of thy young summer prime,
    When can o'er-mast'ring and remorseful Time,
Another send like thee to greatly speak?
Thou dead! forever from the Darien peak
    Thy fame is wafted in sonorous chime,
    And ev'ry nightingale of ev'ry clime,
Warbles thy woe from his enamoured beak;
Thy sweet name 'writ in water?' lo, the years
Of Hero and Leander, all are thine,
    And ev'ry fond maid's breast doth softly swell
Mute kneeling at thy song-embowered shrine;
    Poet, who hath us meshed in magic spell,
Thine the fond tribute of our grateful tears.

SONG

The wind has a mind of its own,
    He's a lover and rover free,
He mutters among the clouds,
    He flutters above the sea;
He ravages regions rare
    Where savages leap in glee,
He strips the forests bare
    In autumnal ecstasy.

The wind is a child of earth,
    Of ocean, air and sky,
He joys at a young world's birth,
    He moans when the old ones die;
He can woo a nodding rose to rest,
    Or trample an empire down,
He's sceptered king of everything,
    And the high stars are his crown.

HEARTH SONG

There's a jingle in the ingle,
   There are forests in the flame,
I see a spark---I hear a lark,
   Warm music without name;
Higher, higher, leaps the fire,
   Hickory, oak or pine,
The songs they heard from every bird,
   This winter night are mine.

Pile the huge logs lovingly,
   Upon the golden blaze,
Higher, higher, friendly fire,
   In praise of happy days;
The storm, the calm, the sun, the wind,
   Gleam glad in every spark,---
O soul, my soul, the living light,
   Doth lurk in living dark.

A SONG FOR YOU

There's a song for you, and a song for me,
   There's a song for everyone;
A song of love or a song of glee,
   Or a song of duty done;
A song by day, and a song by night,
   A song of joy, a song of right;
Let your merry soul with music throng.
Oh, hath your heart its share of song?

The rivers voice a vasty theme,
   Majestic to the sea;
The sentient stars of evening beam
   With mystic melody;
The firmament is glad with mirth,
   Oh, happy, happy, happy earth!
Let music heal the hurt of wrong,
Sing till we have our share of song.

SONG

The world is but a bubble,
　　The stars are little things,
The sea has had a drop too much,
　　I do not care for kings;
Perhaps I do not know them,
　　That may be the reason why;
A little cup turned inside up---
　　The thing we call the sky.

The mountain is a molehill,
　　The molehill is a mount,
　　And hill and mount are of account,
Unto me willy nil;
This little world of little men
　　Is full of little things,
So I rejoice, with feeble voice,
　　And sing my little sings.

SONG

There's a sturdy little fellow,
    Who doth clamber to my knee,
He can prattle, he can yell, O,
    And he thinks a lot of me:
He likes to hear the story
    Of, "Once upon a time,"
And he keeps me ever gory
    With some tragic pantomime.

There's a merry little maiden,
    Who is sister to the chap,
With dolls her arms are laden,
    And she loves them in her lap;
He is sure to be a pirate,
    And sail some Spanish main,
Little sister is a mother,
    And a mother she'll remain.

SONNET

Bereft am I, Urania never-more
Doth come as was her wont to comfort me;
I am undone, sold into slavery,
No more is mine joy's crown ere-while I wore;
Above the curling clouds my song did soar
Undauntedly, in Bacchanalian glee
Brushing her wings in ceaseless ecstasy
Against the patines of the heav'nly floor;
Now all the fountains of the deeps are dry,
Earth, sea and air are cold and desolate,
Urania, Goddess, Queen, wert thou but nigh
My fearless heart might face the frowns of fate;
O spirit of the Muse, once, once again,
Steep me soul deep in wild, undying strain.

SONG

No love have I save Urania,
    No child but the lyric sea,
No hearth and home but the roof-tree dome,
    That shelters the nomads free;
Aroam o'er turban'd desert,
    Or mountain peaks that lie
Their bosoms bare in the upper air
    Aglow with sun and sky.

My heart is a delta basin,
    Fed by a thousand springs,
Where happy herds of lute-voiced birds
    Forever preen their wings;
No woman, save Urania,
    No babes but the waifs of rhyme
Who clamber about, with rout and shout,
    Till I kiss her lips of thyme.

CLINKING THE CANAKIN

The rhymes are read, close up the tomes,
    And lay the verses by,
I drank the sparkling lyrics down,
    And drained the vellums dry;
My soul is saturated,
    Drunken, sunken, through and through,
I reel with rare old Omar,
    Lovelace, Herrick, Suckling, too.

A health to Robert Browning,
    To Tennyson, a score,
And Shelley, Keats, compound of sweets,
    Shall have a dozen more;
Here's looking at you, Byron,
    And some others of the crew,
The wine divine, was thine, 'tis mine,---
    Fill up,---'Tis royal brew.

SONG

Lift up thy voice, and sing,
    Man of love born,
Thou art the king
    Of pity and scorn;
Stars their obeisance make
    Seas share thy unrest,
Hosts of vast passions,
    Rage in thy breast.

Lift up thy voice, and sing,
    Infinite man;
Thou art offspring
    Of portentous plan;
Wrapt all in mystery,
    Breathless, sublime,
Glory confronts thee,
    Heir of all time.

TO R.B.

Robert Browning, Robert Browning,
You're a poet through and through,
Ecstatic and dramatic,
And quite coherent, too;
Pippa passes with the Duchess,
Abt Vogler comes with Saul,
The Piper leads the children,
O we love them one and all;
List now to brave Gallupi
Dreaming o'er his clavichord;
The good Rabbi Ben Esra speaks
Rare wisdom in a word;
Robert Browning, Robert Browning,
Dreamer with a tragic wand,
The mass of men are dunces,
For they never understand;
Magic master of vast music,
Prince of sinuous plot or plan,
Great-hearted, strong and broad of brow,
And all the time a man.

SONG

I know not why I wept so,
   My woe I could not still,
The little breezes crept so
   Softly o'er the hill;
The streamlet sang so cheerly
   It bore my grief away,
I loved them all so dearly,
   I loved them all the day.

I know not why I sang so,
   My joy I could not stay,
The woods that heard me, rang so
   The earth was very gay,
And every little devil
   That prying came about,
Joined in the happy revel,
   And changed into a shout.

ROMEO'S SONG

Juliet, Juliet, dawn is nigh,
    And I must away,
Banish'd, bruisèd, broken,
    Doomed to Mantua;
Child and bride and wife, adieu,
    Fickle and forlorn
Love the tyrant slayeth me,
    Mocketh me in scorn.

Juliet, Juliet, fare thee well,
    Though our hearts are brave,
Thru' the pale mist, sorrow kiss'd,
    The charnel house, the grave;
Juliet, Juliet, once again,---
    Once,---and then away,---
Bruisèd, broken, banish'd,
    I go to Mantua.

JULIET'S SONG

Kiss me, clasp me, hold me fast,
    Fold me from alarm,
The sweetest kisses are the last,
    Fond, and fierce and warm;
Once, then once again, my king,
    Keep me to thy breast,
I, so poor, so slight a thing,
    Thus to be so blest.

Soul, and heart, and bosom flush'd,
    Once, and then again;
The tender night wind, holy, hush'd,
    Moans across the glen;
Quick! the corded stair,---and now,
    Love, my love away,
Dawn must see thee safely,
    Bound for Mantua.

ORLANDO'S SONG

O Rosalind, rare Rosalind,
 'Tis Arden where thou art,
Each tree and leaf bespeak the grief
 And hunger of my heart;
The envious court is left behind,
 And love is monarch here,
The sun, the shade, and everglade,
 Rejoice that thou art near.

O Rosalind, sweet Rosalind,
 My vapid life is vain,
Thou camest by to dye the sky,
 With passion and with pain;
Away with curtle-axe and spear,
 Doff thy assumèd part,
In maiden guise assault mine eyes,
 And captive keep mine heart.

ROSALIND'S SONG

Orlando, my Orlando,
    My name doth mar each tree,
Am I, O love, in sooth, am I,
    The unexpressive She;
Dear heart, dear heart, 'tis Arden
    And in vast content I dwell,
Thy smile, my highest heaven,
    Thy frown, my deepest hell.

Orlando, my Orlando,
    My soul was overthrown,
I gave the chain to voice the pain
    And passion I have known;
The morrow love, shall bring us twain,
Where Hymen waits with all his train,
Deep in love's forest glade to be,
Forever love, with love, and thee.

FERDINAND'S SONG

Tell me sweet, thy name, that I
    May set it in my prayer,
Love, like a bolt from out the sky,
    Hath ta'en me unaware;
A prince am I in mine own clime,
    And thou my queen shalt be,---
O balmy airs of this rare isle,
    That waft such ecstasy.

Out of the wrack of storm and sea,
    I plucked this virgin pearl,
The tempest winds are howling free,
    The fretted billows curl;
Once more, Prospero, wave thy wand
    And dash the dark apart,
Come my Miranda, nestle in
    The harbor of my heart.

MIRANDA'S SONG

By Prospero's magic wand,
The tempest came, and Ferdinand;
Ferdinand, who lights the isle
With the wonder of his smile;
Ferdinand, whose holy vow,
Sets my bosom singing now;
All the ocean and the land,
Cry to me of Ferdinand.

Till thou camest, I was lone,
Love, to me, a zone unknown,
Cast adrift amid the seas
Of the still vex'd Bermoothees;
A father, worthiest of men,
The monster Caliban, and then,---
All sunlight burst upon the strand,
The morning came, and Ferdinand.

OTHELLO'S SONG

O, I have slain my love,
A gull, a dolt, am I,
Look vile Iago, where
My wife doth martyr'd lie;
O, I have slain my love,
A deed unhallow'd done,
Mad and unholy craft,
My soul hath overthrown.

O, I have slain my love,
The sweetest innocent
That ever look'd above
To the brave firmament;
Woe now doth weigh me down
With weary overplus;---
'Twas in Aleppo, once I smote
A damnèd traitor---thus!

DESDAMONA'S SONG

I love thee, cruel Moor,
    So come my soul to bliss,
Weak, innocent and poor,
    I die upon thy kiss;
Steadfast and ever true,
    A child to chiding I;---
My noble lord, adieu,
    A guiltless death I die.

What should I know of sin,
    Who sacred kept my vow,
Treason hath crept within
    To cloud Othello's brow;
I drink the bitter brew,
    It passeth, night is nigh;---
My noble lord, adieu,---
    A guiltless death I die.

CARDENIO
(A Lost Play of Shakespeare)

A city sack'd, a nation or a race
Engulf'd, o'er-whelm'd by vast calamity
Were dire indeed, but can eternity
This message from its master mind replace?
What was the theme? Or warfare brave or base?
What other Juliet with love-lighted eye
And passion pent in every breathèd sigh?
What hero bold, with God-illumined face?
Wrapped in the mummy cloth of mystery,
Lost, gone, evanished in the dusk of years,
And luckless fate has cast away the key
That oped perchance the fountain of all tears;
A magic glass wherein all love, all woe,
All life, all death might lurk,---Cardenio!

THE CHALLENGE

Here are gay skies and butterflies,
    Mab, Oberon, and all the crew,
And courts and kings, and other things,
    And lofty deeds for one to do.

But o'er it all a hazy pall
    Of vague monotony pervades,
I would ten valiant devils now
    Dare front me with their hissing blades!

WE CRAWL, WE CRINGE

We crawl, we cringe. Come, let us leap,
O soul, intrepid be thy sweep.
Perch'd on the lone crag of the day,
The eagle sun holds sov'ran sway.

We yield, we cede. Come, let us fight,
With one world-girdling slogan---right!
Look, where o'er star-still lakes of night,
The swan moon dreams in peaceful flight.

SONG

I.

O New Year be a true year,
    And I'll be true to thee,
The highest goal shall urge my soul,
    In vast sincerity.

II.

O New Year be a true year,
    And I'll be true to thee,
Each word and thought with hope be fraught
    And truth and loyalty.

III.

O New Year and O true year
    I bring my heart to thee,
Up the wide ways of all the days
    Grant peace and love to me.

ON THE WAY TO WILLOWDALE

On the way to Willow-dale,
There are visions in the vale;
Hope, with shining eyes uplighted,
Passion, tense, and pent and pale;
All the ghosts of other days,
All the fairies and the fays
Prank within the woodland ways,
And the cardinal and quail
Whir and whistle o'er the rail
Past the farmer with his flail,---
On the way to Willow-dale.

On the way to Willow-dale,
There are voices in the vale;
"Still pursue, thou can'st not fail,
Hell and death can ne'er prevail;"
If thy heart and soul persist
All the shadow and the mist
Will arise from the skies in thine eyes,
And the dreams of the streams of thy tears
Will come true, and the phantom of fears
Will flee far away in the gray of the day;
On a full tide of fruitage thy galleons sail
To a harbor untouch'd by or tempest or gale,---
On the way to Willow-dale.

THE END.

Sonnets of the Strife

With Songs

With

A FOREWORD BY JOHN BURROUGHS

Originally published in 1917

To
MR. AND MRS. MORTON E. JUDD
and **HUBERT**
with affectionate regard.

FOREWORD

I can gladly stand sponsor for the poetic talent of Robert Loveman. He is a true poet of a rare order, and, though of Hungarian parentage, is a true American.

These poems suggested by the war strike the note we like to hear on this side of the world – the humanitarian, democratic note, and they strike it with vigor attuned to music.

"The kings are going, let them go!" Let every crowned head in Europe roll in the dust, and let the people elect their rulers, and there will be no more war.

Our author's previous work, especially the thin volume called "The Gates of Silence," in which occurs that exquisite lyric, "April Rain," and which any poet in the world might be proud to have written, stamp him as a poet of unusual merit. No other singer of our time has essayed deep-sea soundings into the problems of human destiny and done it with a plumet of four-line stanzas, with great ease and gayety of heart, as has Loveman in his "Gates of Silence." Much of it as good as the best in Omar Khayyam.

In these war poems the martial note is never struck, but only the note of human sympathy and brotherhood. I am sure that is as his readers would have it.

JOHN BURROUGHS – Riverby, West Park, N.Y.

359

CONTENTS

O SET THE NATIONS FREE

Lord God Hosts from out whose hand
    the stars are flung afar,
Our orb is rent with discontent and torn
    with savage war;

Come forth in might majesty and set the
    nations free,
Who grapple to a dismal end in frantic
    ecstasy.

The wreckage of a thousand ships are
    strewn about the seas,
The bombs of death pollute the breath of
    every fragrant breeze;

Lord God thy planet that was fair is gory
    deep in grime,
Our age is one vast blotch of blood upon
    the page of time;

Hast thou no potent opiate where thy
    pavilion swings,
To calm the lust of murder within the
    hearts of kings?

Our joyous earth on tireless wing went
    singing on its way,
The widow's wail, the orphan's cry now
    darken all the day.

Come in thy glory, God, and bid the battle
    sorrows cease,
Pour on the wounds of mangled earth the
    healing oil of peace.

Lord God of Hosts who still hath been our
    buckler and our shield,
To loving bonds of brotherhood let now the
    nations yield.

BROTHERS

O brothers, we are children of the sons of
    man,
Valiant, fearful, haughty, tearful, clinging
    close to class or clan,
Split in sordid, narrow nations, caught in
    creeds that bless or ban,
But brothers, we are brothers of the sons of
    man.

O brothers, we are children of the sons of
    man,
With step elate the millions march upon
    the battle van;
They die like sheep in shambles (dear God,
    send peace again),
O brothers, are we brothers of the sons of
    men?

The fleets of air that journey fair, on joyous
    mission bent,
Now fling their death darts flaming, from
    the fiery firmament;
Where soft the ocean billows breathe, or
    where the breakers swell,
Squat on their hips, the battleships, are
    baying hounds of hell.

O brothers, 'tis the mothers who are
   martyred at the guns,
Europa's soul is stricken with the slaughter
   of her sons,
The great world heart is heavy (dear God
   send peace again),
And brothers still be brothers of the sons of
   men.

THE DEAD SINGER

Here let the wood dove softly coo,
    Here let the willow weep,
Here where the winds and waters woo,
    The singer dreams in sleep.

The music of his magic lute
    Aroused the world to song,
Now that the singer's lips are mute,
    About his bier thy throng.

He hears, he feels, in sleep he smiles,
    Through dusk and dawning dim,
Adown the hushed forest aisles
    They bring their songs to him.

COLUMBIA

COLUMBIA, though all the world doth rage,
Thou art our rock of everlasting peace;

When the grim grapple of the Czars shall cease
And Slav and Teuton stagger from the stage
Bespoiled sisters of shamed age,---

Thy fields shall flower and thy bounds increase
In hereditaments of loving lease;

Oh let thy holy purpose still engage
To be pacificator of all men,

Thy ports the haven of the meek and low,
Thy happy hearthstones ever radiant when
The children gather at the firelight glow;

COLUMBIA! rear thou each loyal son,
Of Lincoln's mould, and mighty Washington.

VENUS AT DAWN

Poor Venus, dying, faint, afar,
Dear paling, fading morning star,
In the gay east there flames a feast
Of fiery light engulfing night,
And you I deemed so lustrous fair
Have perished in the morning air;
Gulp'd down like any tiny mouse
That Wumpus finds about the house;
I came to see a sunrise rare,
With pomp and glory everywhere,---
But vanished Venus, just between us,---
That burly sun cannot bemean us;
Soft;---meet me ere the full blown morn,
We'll hold the blusterer in scorn;
I'll strew thy bier with longings gray,
When thou dost die into the day.

TO THE PRESIDENT

O Pilot of the great ship of our State,
    Thy God sustain thee in this turbid day,
    The wrangling elements beset thy way,
The waters of the world are rife with hate;

O Pilot, some vast purpose of wise fate
    Hath set thee at the helm, and bids thee stay
    Calm, brave, undaunted, until reason's ray
The wrack allay, the tempest dissipate;

O Pilot, thee thy children fond, revere,
    Secure in their firm trust, thou canst ne'er fail
    To weather ev'ry wind and warring gale
Until the harbor of sweet peace be near;

Guide thou the ship of State, majestic, free,
The banners at the mast are Love and Liberty.

SONG

Not in far lands agleam with snow or sun,
Doth paradisial joys exultant lie,
Lo, at thy feet the homely blisses run,
Above thee bends the fold, familiar sky.

Not in the orient or adown the west
Hope, happiness, and fruited peace are found,
At thy warm hearthstone dwell repose and rest,
Thy fragrant garden is the hallowed ground.

WORLD WAR

The kings are going, there will be no kings
    When compt shall come for all this bloody day;
    Out of the carnage and the sanguine fray
Are looming portents of compulsive things;

Vast are the tidings my Marconi brings,
    The heirs of Hapsburg banisht in dismay,
    The Romanovs are fleeing ashen gray,
The children starve, there are bread riotings,

The house of Hohenzollern is laid low,
The kings are going, let them swiftly go;

A stricken world in horror and despair
    Sickens of hate and venomed mutterings.
Of court and clique, and damned intrigue there,
    The kings are going, there must be no kings.

SONG

Give all thou hast, go get thee more,
And still persist in giving;
Give gold, give love, give sympathy,
'Tis very bliss of living;
The flowers freely fragrance breathe,
The seas pour out their store,
Clouds rise and swell upon the skies,
To give, and give the more.

Give all thy mind, give all thou soul,
Give all thy teeming brain,
When thou hast parted with the whole,
The best doth yet remain;
Give all thy days, give all thy years,
Give all thy joy, give all thy tears,
All that thou hast, O mortal give,
This is the only way to live.

WHEN FROM HOARSE GUNS

When from hoarse guns the iron clamor dies,
And tatter'd nations shiver in dismay,
What will be said of this decadent day,
Besotted in its damn'd atrocities?

What must the cynic gods in startled skies
To all this futile, wild alarum say?
The Briton, Turk and Teuton fondly pray
Each for his arms, the winged victories;

Our orphaned age is smit with serried woe,
Art, music, science, lagging at the rear,
Pale pestilence about the field doth go,
Gaunt famine follows with a hungry leer;

O time! O day! O age! a thousand years
Cannot erase the heartache, blood and tears.

THE PLAY

The Play's the thing,
And Life's the play,
The curtain rises
With the day;
Morning is youth,
At noon, a rune of June,
Then manhood's
Mighty afternoon.

The Play's the thing,
Life is the Play,
Lascivious Autumn
Comes in gray,
Mauve, olive, ivory,---
Russet, brown,---
Old gray-beard,
Ring the curtain down.

THE RIVERS

The rivers of war-lands in dismay
Are mournful watchers of distress and woe;
There tenderly the weeping Rhine doth flow
In sympathy upon her wand'ring way;
The tearful Thames arrayed in somber gray
Majestic murmurs requiems soft and low,
The while her sister Seine in grief doth go
Singing in rhythmic sorrow of the fray;
The Danube drinks her dark draught to the lees,
The Neva's breast doth surge with heavy tide,
O woeful hour! in bloody days as these
The savage race of man in shame should hide;
Poor troubled rivers whilst thy children die
How can sun, moon, or stars illume the sky?

POLAND
(1916)

There is a God in Israel,
He seemeth far away
From courts and kings and princes
Who govern us today;
There is a God in Israel,
But what can one God do
With all the frantic bedlam
Of all the crazy crew?

There is a God in Israel,
Sooner or late he comes,
A widowed, orphaned, ravisht peace
Follows the muffled drums;
Dear God who was in Israel,
Come visit us today,---
There is a God in Israel,
He seemeth far away.

INVOCATION

The Sheik-ul-Islam at the Serail Mosque
Prays Mahmud, grace unto the Ottoman;
His brother Teuton fervently doth ask
Herr Gott for habitation neath the sun;

To Le Bon Dieu, the Frenchman fondly cries,
That he may spurn the bold invader forth,
And Albion's sons assail the patient skies
With pleas to God, as much or little worth;

The Maharajas of the golden Ind,
Perturbed folk of ev'ry land and clime,
Send supplication over wave and wind;---
O deities bedazed! O parlous time!

Somewhere perchance, tender or savage prayers
Are treasured by the gods with pitying tears

SONG

I thank thee, God, that I was strong,
    That life leap'd lusty in my blood,
For ev'ry thrush or linnet song,
    For love and all our nestling brood.

I bless thee, God, that I am old,
    And bent and poor, and weak and blind.
I drained the chalices of gold,
    Firmly I face the leaden wind.

THE WORLD IS MAD

The world is mad, the nations are insane,
Stark bedlam reigns o'er half the frantic earth,
The womb of Time doth give prodigious birth
To monstrous deeds upon the land and main;

The frowning hosts of Mars have all the gain,
Our smiling arts of peace have little worth;---
Banisht the soft designs of joyous mirth,
Europa, frenzied, writhes in tragic pain!

COLUMBIA, be thou steadfast, patiently
With love and pity view the startling fray;
Saints, villains, heroes, all commingled be
In the death-grapple for world mastery;

Dear God, speed thou the most auspicious day,
When Might shall lay his boastful power away.

THE PLAY

The throngs that jostle in the street,
Are people in a play,
The tragic and the humorous,
The grievous and the gay;
Youth and doddering dotard,
Moonlight, storm or sun,
Ring up the magic curtain,
The play has just begun.

Sweet melodies insistent
Pervade the *mise en scène*,
Sunshine clothed in shadow,
Snow white or willow green;
Heroes, clowns and villain,
Dusk drowns the weary sun,---
Ring down the twilight curtain,
The play of life is done.

WHAT WILL EVOLVE?

What will evolve from out this hellish strife,
The loot, the pillage, and the mad rapine?
Some final good, some lofty goal serene,
Must be for all who inherit life.

What world-wide sunlit revolution rife
Of liberty and love doth lurk unseen?
The body-politic is foul, unclean,
The fester splutters to the surgeon's knife.

Perchance the peasant and the toiler low,
May rise to stature of enfranchised men,
Europa's humble millions soon may know
Fair freedom breaking over bog and fen.

If it be so, dear God, not all in vain,
The vast procession of the maimed and slain.

SONG

Leaf of the tree, wave of the sea,
Beam of the star, and breezes free,
Light of the morn, grace of the thorn,
How can the bosom feel forlorn?
The lush warm grass, and birds that pass,
Love of the lad, faith of the lass,
Over us all the sun's bright eye,
In the blue of the summer sky.

Bower, tower, flower and hour,
Dower of health, fame and power,
Charity, hope, and peace and rest,
Thrilling with joy the eager breast,
The day and night in happy flight,
The noon of June, a dream delight,
And life and death a joyous song,
For him who knows not hate nor wrong.

TO HENRY FORD

When the grim war lords and their jealousies
Are buried with the muck and trash of time,
Thy dream that came immortal and sublime
Shall still illume the blood-stained centuries;

The little men make mock of lofty deed,
The gun-men vend their iron chattel still,
One beam doth gleam while all the world doth bleed,
Thy light of love set on hope's highest hill;

Be undismayed, the dream shall yet avail,
Nations unborn will laud thy peaceful prayer,
The craft sent forth into the hateful gale
Will anchor in fame's harbor calm and fair;

O strive again, beyond the tumult's rage,
Hist'ry for thee shall keep her whitest page.

WILLOW SONG

Willow, willow, in the spring,
When my heart is hungering,
First of all thou then art seen
In a shimmering gown of green,
Then full soon that thou art found,
Thy garments trailing to the ground.
Do dryads deem thee, flowing there,
An emerald fountain in the air?
Ne'er a willow weeps for me,
Thou gracile, verdant ecstasy,
But in rapt beauty thou dost gleam,
O'er the meadow, by the stream;
Willow, willow, in the spring,
When my heart is hungering.

SONNET

Now that the eve is tranquil, calm, and still,
Now that the goal I sought in youth, finds me,
Now that the benison of rock and tree,
The comrad'ry of valley and of hill
With a vast surge of sympathy doth thrill
My soul to overflow, and every sea
Murmurs again an olden melody,---
The dawn doth prophesy, and dusk fulfill;
Beach'd in the port of peace my heart doth dwell,
War's tumult seems an eager infant's play,
I watch, I wait, my peaceful beads I tell,
While down the west recedes majestic day;
O Youth, O Love, O Age, the world is fair,
Host upon host of glories throng the air.

SPRING SONG

A balmy hint, then from the mint
   Of April comes a flood
Of dandelion riches,
   Making opulent the wood;
They cluster in a fluster---
   How good the grasses feel!
The Crœsus Spring his gold doth fling,
   The winter's hurt to heal.

The daffodils are redolent
   With hope and happiness,
The jonquils beatific
   In a becoming dress;
The mellow, yellow flowers
   Make a fellow feel benign;
I owe no debt of vain regret---
   Old Midas' store is mine.

SONNET

Great themes and deeds surge o'er me, I stand lone
On Pisgah gazing to the promised land,
Or on the banisht, bleak, Helena strand,
Looking to seaward with Napoleon.

The airs of Egypt waft my galleon
Where Cleopatra lies by houris fanned,
Or at a statue's base I stricken stand
And find the mighty Cæsar, bleeding, prone;

A vast procession of immortal men
And gorgeous women come within my ken;
O Life, I cry, what art thou, where dost lead?
Where are these restless souls, and where shall I
Quitting the hill-top and the pleasing mead,
Is it but death,---or life anew to die?

FOR WORSHIP ALL THE DAY

Every tree's a shrine to me,
Each rock a temple rare,
Each holy nook by hill or brook
Is dedicate to prayer;
Along go song with every hour,
And flower by the way,
Each sacred space is time and place
For worship all the day.

Every star doth gleam afar
On altar of the night;
The priestess moon in silver shoon
Doth bless each peaceful light;
Anon the dawn doth bloom again,
The east in glad array,---
Up valiant, happy heart and strong,
For worship all the day.

OUR DAYS

Our days are not for puny men or things,
    For pigmy thought or idle prose or rhyme,
    Blazoned upon the red shield of our time,
Behold the death throes of the grappling kings;

War's cauldrons hot with hated venomings,
    Europa clad in bloody garb of grime,
    Her sons steeped deep in filth, disease, and slime
Mid livid guns' tumultuous thunderings;

A creeping, crawling, cringing peace then comes
Behind the bluster of the blatant drums;

There is no God in battle; Satan's throne
    Is builded by the souls who cherish war,
Hell groans with music of the dying moan,
    Its mad dominion all one hid'ous scar.

SONG

I'm weary with the war, I'll to my gardens go,
And watch the blossoms and the buds ablow;

I'm sick of strife, I'll love the lilac more,
And gay wisteria shall adorn my door;

I'm neutral, let the foolish fight, who will,
For me wild flower flags wave on the hill;

I am a non-combatant and I see
Ahead of me a violet victory.

I'm weary of the war, peace I declare,
Of spoil and possession I demand no share.

Hark! Lo, a redbird in the green wood tree,
His song the pæan of delight for me.

SONG

Sing in the morning,
And sing in the night;
Sing away scorning,
And sing in delight;
Sing away sorrow,
And sing away slight,
Tomorrow, tomorrow,
Thy woes may laugh light.

Sing on, and sing ever,
Heart of my heart,
Shadow shall never
Grieve us apart;
Sing to me, cling to me,
Heart of my heart,
Sing 'til it bring to me
Love, and love's art.

WITH FORGIVING TEARS

When Zepp'lins have laid London waste, then must
    Berlin the beautiful surely go;
    Edith Cavell, sweet martyr saint, doth know
High Heaven is but for those who love and trust;

Foremost among the phalanx of the just,
    Who for ideals strike heroic blow,
    The bold Knight Casement doth immortal show,
His proud soul rising from melodious dust;

Brave Fryatt follows, at the dawn of day
He mounts heroic to the stars away;

When frantic man has spent his futile rage
    Upon his brother, and the book of fears
Is closed, dear God, seal thou the page
    Of sorrow with forgiving tears.

O MY BROTHERS!

O my brothers gaunt and grappling to the
    death across the sea,
Every wave of ocean bears the woe and sorrow
    unto me;
O my brothers is not life and all the sunlight
    fair?---
O my brothers, blinded, bruised, broken
    everywhere.

O my brothers of the old world across the
    yearning sea,
The horror and the pity of the struggle comes
    to me;
Hath not God unto us given earth to be a
    garden fair?---
And the tribes of neighbor nations crying,
    dying everywhere.

O my brothers, Turk or Teuton, Anglo-Franco,
    Russ or Hun,
Children of the old earth mother, sired at the
    morning sun;
Is there ne'er an end to strife and murder
    darkening the air?---
With God's vast and kindly presence pleading
    sweet peace everywhere.

AMERICA

The fairest land, the rarest land,
   The land we love the best,
Is our own land that staunch doth stand
   A tower in the west;
An ocean wide on either side,
   The gulf beneath her feet,
The very name, AMERICA,
   Doth make our pulses beat.

The sweetest land, the fleetest land,
   The land where freedom dwells
Is our own land of mountains,
   And clover covered dells;
One joyous, vast Republic,
   God! how we cherish her,
The very name, AMERICA,
   Doth make our bosoms stir.

AMERICA, AMERICA,
   O may we die for thee,
Proclaiming unto all the earth
   Our love of liberty;
AMERICA, AMERICA,
   Our banner is unfurled,
Thy pæan of democracy
   Shall ring about the world.

THE END.

ABOUT THE AUTHOR

Robert Loveman was born in Cleveland, Ohio on April 11, 1864. He was educated at the Dalton Academy in Dalton, Georgia. Loveman would spend many years of his life in Dalton. After attending the Dalton Academy, Loveman continued his studies at the University of Alabama ultimately receiving his Master of Arts. While attending school in Tuscaloosa, he stayed with relatives at the Battle Friedman House. During his time at the house, Loveman wrote much of his most popular works including a poem that would later become the official state song of Georgia before being replaced by *Georgia on My Mind* in 1979.

Loveman's *Rain Song (page 151)* , or *April Rain*, became very well known. It inspired the Al Jolson song "April Showers." Though, it must be noted that Loveman filed suit against Jolson for infringement. The case was dropped after the death of Loveman on July 10, 1923 in Hot Springs, Arkansas. Al Jolson would later appear in the first full-length motion picture with synchronized dialogue, *The Jazz Singer*.

Robert Loveman is buried in West Hill Cemetery in his beloved Dalton, Georgia.

Made in the USA
Columbia, SC
06 October 2021